CHURCH GROWTH PRINCIPLES

Separating Fact from Fiction

C. KIRK HADAWAY

BROADMAN PRESS
NASHVILLE, TENNESSEE

Library of Congress Cataloging-in-Publication Data

Hadaway, C. Kirk
  Church growth principles : separating fact from fiction / C. Kirk
Hadaway.
    ISBN 0-8054-6014-4
    1. Church growth--United States--Baptists. 2. Southern Baptist
Convention--Membership. 3. Baptists--United States--Membership.
    I. Title.
BR526.H22
254'.5--dc20   90-41228
                                                                    CIP

Church Growth Principles

Contents

List of Figures

Introduction

There are almost as many church growth principles as there are growing churches in America. Each book published by a "card-carrying" member of the church growth movement or by one of its "fellow travelers" contains dozens of such principles. Unfortunately, most of these principles, keys, vital signs, and steps to church growth are simply hunches. They are often based on careful observation and are usually plausible, but they have not been tested or verified.

Church-growth literature is based largely on observations of rapidly growing churches. Case studies have been collected and models developed illustrating how certain churches "did it" or at least how they think they did it. Books lift up such churches as Coral Ridge Presbyterian; Willow Creek Community Church; Melodyland Christian Center; First Baptist, Dallas; First Baptist, Hammond; Garden Grove Community Church; Yoido Full Gospel Church; and others as examples of how massive growth is possible. The implication is that they did it, so you can, too, if you follow their methods. More analytical church growth studies have gone a bit further in trying to find similarities in the growth strategies of such churches and have presented these similarities as principles or even "laws" of church growth.

The case study has its place as a legitimate research technique, but it is best used as a supplement to more rigorous research procedures which allow growth hypotheses to be tested. Used alone, case studies may give a distorted view of how churches grow. They represent a classic example of what one sociologist has called the "offbeat group fallacy." The knee-jerk strategy of amateur researchers who are interested in some unusual group is to do case studies or surveys just among that population. If they want to understand growing churches, they either conduct case studies of the fastest-growing churches, or they do a survey among them.

The problem with studying an unusual group, like the fastest-growing churches in America, is that the researcher has no way of knowing whether or not the characteristics they share are any different from the characteristics of churches which are not growing. Further, such research provides no way of knowing which church growth-producing factor is more important than any other.

Church-growth writers may assume that they are only too familiar with the characteristics of plateaued and declining churches because most churches in America are not growing rapidly. Thus, they are easily able to discriminate those factors which are unique to the fastest growing churches. This assumption may be valid to some extent, but the fact remains that such casual judgments may not always be accurate and are incapable of determining the relative power of various church-growth principles.

Another problem with traditional church-growth research is that it is too dependent on the extremes. The largest churches and the fastest-growing churches receive all of the attention. Will information about these churches help the average church grow? Most churches have the opportunity for growth, but few have the potential to become another Crystal Cathedral. It may well be that the strategies used by the fastest-growing churches in America are not the most feasible strategies for achieving renewed growth in most small congregations. Up to this point, however, there has been no way of knowing.

The leadership in one dynamic church may say that their growth is largely the result of a bus ministry. And, in fact, the bus ministry may have worked for them. But what about the thousands of other churches which use bus ministries for outreach? Does it work for them also? Are churches which use bus ministries for outreach more likely to grow than churches which do not have them? Case studies of growing congregations cannot answer these questions, but there are other research techniques which can.

Research findings from an extensive church-growth survey among Southern Baptist churches have revealed that growing churches are no more likely to use bus ministries than are plateaued and declining churches. There is absolutely no relationship between church growth and presence or absence of a bus ministry.

The wonderful thing about many church growth theories which have been proposed is that they are testable using modern research techniques. Unfortunately, much more effort has gone into publishing church growth theories and presenting them as facts, than has gone into actually testing these theories. The purpose of this book is to report the results of efforts to test a wide variety of church-growth hypotheses. A further purpose is to show which growth-related principles are more important than others. Using statistical procedures it is possible, for example, to show whether evangelistic efforts are correlated with church growth, and if so, whether or not they are more or less important to growth than goal setting, length of pastor tenure, pastor-leadership style, or population growth in the community.

One thing the reader will not find in this book is a biblical justification for church growth. I am not a theologian, and even if I was, this sort of exercise has been done more than adequately in other books. Conservative, evangelical denominations are committed to growth. Pastors and denominational leaders believe that, in general, growth is good and decline is to be avoided whenever possible. Growth represents success in efforts to "evangelize and congregationalize." Not all growth is seen as "authentic," and it is recognized that many churches grow through the evangelistic efforts of others rather than through efforts of their own. Nevertheless, growth is positive and to be encouraged.

In denominations which place less stress on evangelism, declines over the past two decades have led to a renewed interest in church growth. Gone are the arguments that such denominations are losing only the deadwood and are being reduced to a committed core. They have begun to realize that even their core has become less committed and has been peeling away in rather thick layers.

Despite the recognition that growth is desperately needed in mainline denominations, the sentiment remains that rapid growth is somehow tainted, as if the pastors of such churches had to give up something important in order to achieve it. If nothing else, the pastors of growing churches must be ignoring the spiritual well-being of their members, sacrificing worship for entertainment, and substituting promotion for ministry. This widespread belief has been found to be untrue, however. Recent research into the correlates of "growth in mature faith" and "effective Christian education" has shown that adults in growing churches tend to indicate more growth in faith on the average than do adults in churches which are not growing. Growing churches also were found to exhibit greater overall levels of strength and effectiveness in other areas of church life, such as worship, congregational warmth, quality of the Christian education program, spiritual development, congregational loyalty, and social-service orientation.

One of the presuppositions of this book is that, in general, church growth is a "good thing." It is a view which has been supported theologically, ethically, and statistically (although not without arguments to the contrary). But proving or even substantiating this presupposition is not my purpose. I leave that to theologians. Growth will be treated as a goal which churches, as organizations, deem to be important. Accepting this goal as valid, the questions become, "what factors are associated with growth, and what factors are associated with decline?" Also, "what growth-producing factors are of greatest importance?" To answer these questions with the best objective, scientific research available is the purpose of this book.

Many data sources will be used to answer the questions which have been posed. The most critical source is a large-scale church growth survey which was conducted among over five hundred metropolitan Southern Baptist churches in 1988. This survey, which was sent to selected of pastors in rapidly growing churches, plateaued churches, and declining churches was designed to test a wide variety of church growth hypotheses, drawn from many sources.

Another major source of data for this book is a survey of Southern Baptist churches on the plateau, which was also conducted in 1988. The purpose of this research was to compare the characteristics of churches which had grown off the plateau with the characteristics of churches which remained on statistical plateaus. The intent was to test various theories and hypotheses for how stagnant churches can reverse longstanding trends and begin to grow.

In addition to these recent studies, I will look at previous efforts to test church-growth hypotheses conducted in a variety of settings—including denominations other than the Southern Baptist Convention. One of these was a large-scale study of United Presbyterian churches which was conducted in 1975 as part of a larger effort to understand the membership losses being suffered by most liberal and moderate mainline denominations in the 1970s. Another similar effort, which took place about the same time was a study of United Church of Christ congregations conducted by William McKinney, who directed research for the United Church of Christ at that time.

In addition to these large-scale efforts to examine church-growth theories, this book will also draw upon a number of more limited projects. Included among these are a study by Clay Price of growing, highly evangelistic churches; my work on the influence of church settings in Memphis; and a number of other useful studies.

It is not the purpose of this book to criticize any particular person or school of thought. In other words, this book is not an attack on the church-growth movement as it has evolved from the writings of Donald McGavran. There are many good books which have come out of this school of thought, and writers such as Peter Wagner, Charles Chaney, Kent Hunter, and Charles Arn have a great deal of insight into why churches grow in the American setting. At the same time, many of the authors within this tradition are so tied to McGavran's church-growth theory as an *ideology* that they accept all it contains uncritically. This is a hindrance to the movement which they seek to foster because it prevents objective evaluation of the theory. As a result, no systematic effort has been made within the church-growth movement to examine its presuppositions, principles, and "laws" through the use of modern, objective, research techniques.

There is truth in the church-growth literature, but there is undoubtedly error. For this reason, the approach taken in this book is that everyone's theory of church growth is open to question, including my own. Nothing is sacred, not the writings of Donald McGavran, Peter Wagner, Lyle Schaller, or even those within my own agency of the Southern Baptist Convention who may feel that they found the keys to church growth long ago (certainly before Donald McGavran laid claim to the term). If the theories are testable, regardless of who developed the theories, I have tried to test them or find research which has done so.

The book is organized into twelve chapters, each dealing with important church-growth concerns. The first chapter, for instance, considers publicity, evangelism training, prospect visitation, prospect files, programmed-evangelism campaigns, special-emphasis days, area crusades and simultaneous revivals, the extent of church involvement in evangelistic activity, and a number of other issues. The chapter on Sunday

School and small groups deals with the overall emphasis on Sunday School in a church; the vitality of the Sunday School program for singles, couples, and youth; the use of outreach leaders, workers' meetings, teacher training, Sunday School visitation, and enrollment procedures; and techniques for starting new classes.

In addition to chapters dealing with church programs and leadership, several chapters deal with growth-related activities and characteristics. Do planning and goal setting encourage growth? This question is addressed in chapter 6. How do growing churches attract visitors, make them feel welcome and accepted, convince them to join, assimilate them into the life of the church, hold on to them, and then get them back if they should drop out? These important issues are discussed in chapters 7 and 8.

Additional chapters deal with innovation, the need for spirituality and ministry, and the community setting. Are growing churches innovative or traditional, is spiritual renewal necessary to lead churches off the plateau, and what is the role of the church setting in facilitating or stymieing efforts to grow? Chapters 9 through 11 attempt to answer these and other questions, among others.

The last chapter is titled, "The Primary Principles." Here all of the key influences on church growth are considered together, using sophisticated statistical procedures, in order to determine which factors are of primary importance to the growth of a church. Specifically, this chapter attempts to answer the question of how well various growth-related factors discriminate rapidly growing churches from plateaued and declining churches. This chapter serves as a conclusion to the book and will allow church professionals to distinguish what is essential from what is merely helpful as they seek to lead their churches to renewed or continued growth.

Many people have helped this book become a reality. Particular thanks is due to two close friends who saved me from disasters of various types: Penny Long Marler and Bill Peter. Penny pointed out my logical inconsistencies, frequent blind biases, and a few incomprehensible sentences. She also contributed substantially to my comments on the role of the pastor and laity in planning for change. Bill saved me on several occasions by recreating lost data files and by performing all sorts of file manipulation and merging. I am in their debt.

1
Outreach and Evangelism

For the vast majority of churches in the United States, growth does not come easily, if it comes at all. Great effort is required, channeled toward goals which produce growth, rather than dissipated through other activities which are quite worthy but are unrelated to their growth.

There are more than enough sermons, meetings, funerals, zoning hearings, weddings, hospital visits, and various crises to fill a pastor's week far beyond forty hours. Similarly, the ongoing business of running a church can keep active lay members too busy to take on anything else. Yet growth will not occur by simply keeping the machine oiled and running. It must be going somewhere if growth is the destination; and this takes a strategy which ensures that growth-producing activities are an integral part of the ongoing work of the pastor and laity.

Apparently, one of these necessary activities is outreach. In order for a church to grow, members must be engaged in efforts to attract and persuade nonmembers to visit and join the congregation. Without such efforts, a church may have good things to offer, but few will hear about them. Consequently, growth is unlikely.

Evangelism is a form of outreach. Churches may try to attract anyone they can, without necessarily trying to win anyone to Christ. This is not evangelism, but it is outreach or recruitment. Most books on church growth talk more about evangelism than recruitment, but it is likely that both are related to membership growth.

Outreach and Church Growth: The Basic Relationship

Church growth experts universally list evangelism as a major church growth principle. However, very little research has been conducted to determine whether outreach and evangelism, in fact, *do produce growth* or to determine which *types of outreach* might be most effective. Nevertheless, a strong relationship between evangelism and church growth has seemed particularly plausible because in recent years denominations which appear to emphasize aggressive outreach have been growing, while groups which have neglected this sort of activity have been in decline.

The shock of seeing membership losses for the first time in their histories led several denominations to conduct research projects in the mid 1970s to determine why and how mainline churches grow (or decline). One of these projects was conducted by the United Presbyterian Church.

Rather than dealing with evangelism *per se*, the Presbyterian study looked at *recruitment efforts* and showed, in general, rather weak relationships between measures of recruitment activity and church growth. The strongest relationship was produced by the question, "Overall, to what extent are members of your congregation involved in recruiting new members?" In the survey, 45 percent of the growing churches responded "extensively" or "moderately" to this question, as compared to 31 percent of the declining churches.[1]

This relatively modest relationship came as something of a surprise to the investigators. Were recruitment and evangelism *not* strongly related to church growth, or was there some other explanation for the survey results? In order to examine this question (and many others), a church-growth survey was conducted in 1988 among metropolitan Southern Baptist churches.

Survey results showed that 70 percent of *growing* metropolitan Southern Baptist churches reported that their members were extensively or moderately involved in recruitment (as compared to only 45 percent in the Presbyterian study). In the Southern Baptist Convention, 41 percent of plateaued churches and 39 percent of declining churches also reported extensive or moderate involvement in recruitment.

The relationship between recruitment activity and church growth obviously was much stronger among Southern Baptist churches than it was among United Presbyterian congregations. The question to be asked is "why?"

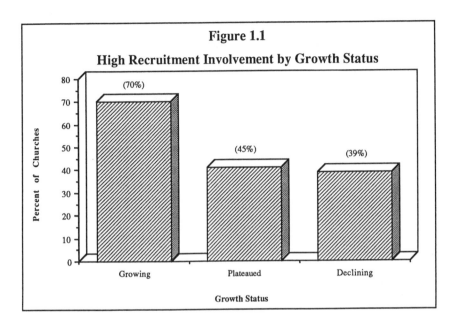

Figure 1.1

High Recruitment Involvement by Growth Status

It may be that recruitment efforts are less effective in reaching potential Presbyterians than in reaching potential Baptists. However, it would appear that the relationship between recruitment and evangelism among United Presbyterian congregations was *artificially reduced* by including churches in their growing category which were plateaued. This suggests that recruitment efforts are important to church growth in *both* liberal and conservative denominations. Further, it seems that it is the effort to reach those outside the church which is critical, not whether the action has an evangelistic thrust. In the Southern Baptist church-growth survey, growing churches were much more likely to say that their members were involved in recruitment *and* evangelism. The relationship with growth was strong for each of them.

It should be remembered, however, that the goal of church growth should be to gain members from the ranks of the unchurched, rather than from other congregations. Churches can grow simply by attracting Christians to a better show and all growing churches will tend to gain members from less vital congregations. However, this type of growth is less important to the kingdom of God than is growth through reaching the lost.

Just how strongly are outreach and evangelism related to church growth? A total of fourteen questions on the church-growth survey were combined to form an outreach/evangelism scale. Questions included in this scale dealt with evangelistic activity, recruitment, evangelism campaigns, visitation, mass mailouts to community residents, evangelism training, and other outreach issues. All churches received a score on the scale, which was collapsed into five categories, ranging from low to high evangelism.

As can be seen in figure 1.2, 42 percent of the growing churches scored high on the evangelism/outreach scale, as compared to only 11 percent of the plateaued churches and 6 percent of the declining churches. A *very* strong relationship exists between outreach and church growth, as shown in this figure. The relationship is a little odd, however.

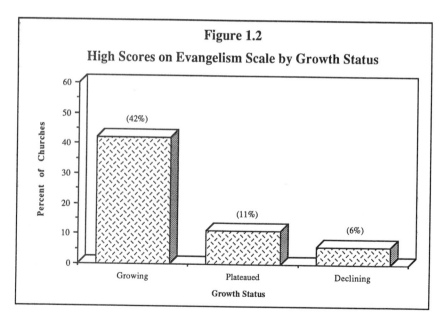

Figure 1.2

High Scores on Evangelism Scale by Growth Status

The difference between growing churches and plateaued churches is huge (31 percentage points), but the difference between plateaued churches and declining churches is small with respect to their outreach score (only 5 percentage points). *Evangelism and outreach characterizes growing churches.* On the other hand, plateaued churches are not very evangelistic on average, nor are declining churches. If they were evangelistic, perhaps they would be growing. Whatever factors distinguish plateaued churches from declining churches must be found in activities other than evangelism.

Growing churches tend to have it all, evangelism, outreach, good Sunday Schools, ministry to the community, and the rest. What does it take to "bump" a stagnant church off its plateau to this level? Additional research has shown that renewed involvement in evangelism is one of the keys to "breakout growth."

In recent survey, churches which experienced rapid growth after six years on the plateau (breakout growth) were compared to churches which still remained on the plateau. The single largest difference between the two sets of churches was evangelistic activity. In most cases a new pastor came to the church and led the congregation to begin to "re-reach" the community for Christ. To grow off the plateau, business as usual will not work. Something *different* is required, and perhaps the most important *one thing* which can be done differently is to restore evangelistic outreach to the life of a church.

If Outreach Is So Important . . .

Even though many evangelistic churches exist in the Southern Baptist Convention, outreach and evangelism are not the major sources of growth for this denomination. Despite misleading statistics taken from the Uniform Church Letter[2] which suggest that SBC churches gain more members from the "outside" than they lose, national survey data has shown that the primary source of growth for the Southern Baptist Convention is the addition of children of existing church members— what has been called "biological growth" by writers in the church-growth tradition.[3]

Southern Baptists have a relatively high birth rate; their members are more committed on average (and thus are more likely to attend and support their churches) than are members of mainline Protestant denominations; and Baptists hold onto their youth better than any other Protestant group (only Catholics and Jews have higher rates of retention). Without a high birth rate and a high rate of retention, the Southern Baptist Convention would decline because more Baptists drop out of the church than are won from the ranks of the "nones," and more Baptists switch to other denominations than are gained.[4]

This does not sound like an evangelistic denomination, and in fact, it isn't, because Southern Baptists *talk* more about evangelism than they *do* evangelism. Evangelism is part of Southern Baptist mythology. Evangelism is sometimes falsely used to explain the denomination's growth.

The image of the Southern Baptist Convention as an evangelistic denomination is maintained by worship services which end in an altar call. Churches rely on pastors as the evangelistic anglers, casting their lines into the congregational pool, which hopefully contains a few "uncaught fish." The occasional parade of "decisions" helps Southern Baptists believe that their church is providing an effective evangelical witness to the community, and if the church is growing, the perception becomes complete and compelling.

For many suburban churches, aggressive outreach is unnecessary for growth. They can rely on their location, population growth through new housing, and the children of members to produce a seemingly healthy growth rate.[5] Unfortunately, by the time population growth in the surrounding community ends and adult members are no longer having children, the church has *long since* lost its ability to do effective outreach. The members do not know how to do it, because they never *had* to do it.

Most churches do some type of visitation through Sunday School, and their pastors may visit a few prospects each week, but evangelistic outreach is rarely a priority in most Southern Baptist Churches in terms of *amount of effort or budget.* Outreach, unlike some other church functions, does not happen from week to week because there is an evangelism committee, or even a minister of evangelism. It is easy *not* to do evangelism, and most churches neglect it until they require outreach in order to grow. By this time it may be nearly too late to mobilize a settled congregation.

Of course, there are some very evangelistic churches in the Southern Baptist Convention. They are typically led by pastors for whom witnessing to non-Christians is not just a priority, it is an aching need. These churches have become particularly effective in reaching the lost and in reclaiming church dropouts because they have combined their evangelistic zeal with efficient organizational procedures which expand the number of members involved in outreach. They have multiplied the avenues of outreach beyond the traditional one-night-per-week visitation and have ensured that all involved in outreach understand how to effectively share their faith with non-Christians. Effective outreach which results in growth also requires a church to disciple and retain its converts, rather than simply recording decisions for Christ. This takes planning, organization, and usually an effective use of Sunday School.

Techniques of Outreach: Visitation

How does a church become evangelistic? The *desire* to reach others for Christ is latent among the members in nearly all churches, but it must be mobilized and channeled into action—especially in the form of prospect visitation. Few members will visit prospects on their own initiative or without the active support of the larger congregation of members.

Visitation is emphasized in Sunday School growth campaigns, in witness training programs, and in most books on church growth. It is one of Kennon Callahan's twelve keys to an effective church; Larry Lewis says, "organized visitation is a must"; Lyle Schaller calls visitation, "the second most effective single approach to evangelism today"; and Paul Powell explained the growth of his church through visitation, "People don't just walk into our church . . . They come because we first go out to visit them."[6]

Most Southern Baptist churches do some form of visitation, even if it only involves occasional prospect visits by the pastor and by a few unusually committed Sunday School teachers. Do most growing churches have a visitation program? The answer is "yes," but so do most declining churches. For this reason, it is hard to *measure* the impact of visitation on church growth using survey methods. To get around this problem a question was devised which asked about "a definite, regular visitation program," which was followed by a question on how often the program was conducted.

As can be seen in figure 1.3, 76 percent of growing churches conduct a visitation program at least weekly, as compared to 51 percent of plateaued churches, and 44 percent of declining churches. Given the loose definition of a visitation program held by many churches, this was a quite strong relationship. Some churches are able to grow without organized visitation programs, but the vast majority of growing churches use visitation as a source of growth. It is a characteristic which tends to separate growing churches from churches which are not growing.

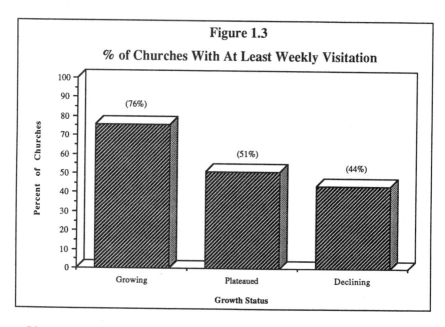

Figure 1.3

% of Churches With At Least Weekly Visitation

If prospect visitation and church growth are related, the next question is: "how should visitation be organized and implemented in order to achieve maximum results?" There is no easy answer to this question because so many options exist. One key strategy, however, relates to prospects.

Growing churches are more likely to maintain "an active, up-to-date prospect file" than are plateaued and declining churches. Also, figure 1.4 shows that churches which have high baptisms *and* rapid growth are much more likely to use prospect files in their weekly visitation than are high baptism/low growth churches or the typical Southern Baptist church (control group in the chart).[7]

Keeping a prospect file organized and up-to-date is a lot of work, but it is essential to an effective visitation program for any congregation. An efficient system ensures that people who sign visitor cards at the worship service or Sunday School receive a visit quickly and that viable

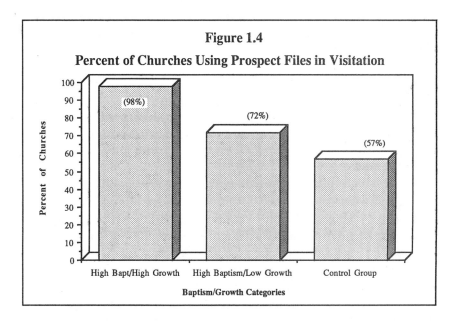

Figure 1.4

Percent of Churches Using Prospect Files in Visitation

prospects are given sufficient attention. It also identifies persons who are not Christians so that they can receive visits by persons who know how to give a clear presentation of the gospel in a nonthreatening manner.

People are impressed when they are visited the day after they attend a new church, and in interviews with new members in growing churches, this point is mentioned frequently. A visit shows that the church cares.

Survey findings suggest that growing churches are more likely to visit new residents in the community, to visit persons who attend their worship services for the first time, to have conducted a religious census in the community, and to have sent out a brochure or other mass mailouts about their church to community residents. These activities are not *essential* for growth, but they *are* related to growth and appear to work for many churches.

Another key to effective visitation is pastor and staff involvement. While there is apparently no "magic number" of visits by the pastor which allows a church to grow, some guidelines can be suggested. In general, more visitation is better than less, with five *prospect* visits per week by the pastor being an absolute minimum in order to maintain growth in a healthy church. For a church on the plateau which desires to grow, the number of prospect visits should be increased to at least ten. If a church has more than one ministerial staff, the minimum number of visits should be raised to at least ten per week for maintenance growth. Breakout growth would require even higher number of visits.

Lewis recommends fifteen prospect visits by the pastor per week, while Callahan suggests twenty for both pastor and laity (in a church of average size).[8]

There is, of course, some small danger of a congregation viewing visitation as "what we hire the staff for." It is more likely, however, that the highly visible symbol of the pastor and staff visiting prospects and leading men and women to Christ will show the laity that the staff sees evangelism as an integral part of their roles as ministers and as a natural part of their lives as Christians. With such role models it is less difficult to involve the laity in the process.

Some would say visitation is a less effective method of outreach today than it was in the past. Gaining entrance to apartment buildings and planned residential communities with guards and (or) security gates makes visitation more of a *challenge* in cities today than it was in small-town America or still is in sprawling single-family suburban developments. Yet, those who say visitation is less effective usually mean "cold-turkey," unannounced, house-to-house, apartment-to-apartment, or trailer-to-trailer visitation—which has never been a very *efficient* method of church growth. The concept of visitation should be expanded beyond showing up at someone's front door for an appointment or an unannounced visit. In fact, in an urban setting, meeting someone for lunch may be more appropriate than visiting them at home. Similarly, talking to homeless persons on a street corner or making a point to talk to an unchurched friend during a break at work, at the health club, at the grocery store, over coffee, or across the back fence can be, and should be, seen as prospect visitation.

Prospect visitation is more difficult in some settings than in others, but in *any* setting, greater success results from visiting prospects who are already linked to the church or to church members in some way. Clearly, the best prospects are those who have already visited the church. If a church is not visiting these persons, it is literally begging to decline. Churches which have few visitors should start with those they do have and develop ways to attract others. Invitations from friends, a telemarketing campaign, radio or television spots, mass mailouts, revivals, a "friend day" or other special event, parenting seminars, a singing Christmas tree, and various forms of social ministry can all be used to draw visitors and develop a list of viable prospects. The names are wasted, however, if they are not followed up *quickly.*

The unchurched parents of children who are attending Sunday School can be another source of prospects. Yet, as James Kennedy notes, "this source . . . will not prove very fruitful unless Sunday School teachers have had an active program of visiting in the homes and showing an interest in the children's progress in their Christian education."[9] And it should be added that an expression of interest in the parents' needs also should be part of such visitation.

New residents in the community are another productive source of prospects, when they are visited quickly. Studies have shown that moving to a new city is associated with changes in religious identity. People who move are more likely to switch denominations, drop out of the church altogether, or convert to a new religious faith.[10] If a church wants to reach "hard-core" unchurched (about 8 percent of the population), targeting new residents is the most effective method for doing so.[11] Such a strategy also helps prevent members of one's own denomination from using the move to a new community as an opportunity to drop out of the church.

Finally, there is house-to-house visitation, or more accurately, housing unit-to-housing unit visitation. Rather than sending church members to witness to every family in an area, a religious census should be conducted first. This produces a list of prospects which can be classified and visited later by someone from the church who lives in the area and who can spend as much time as is required talking to each prospect. Unchurched individuals can be visited by persons who feel comfortable sharing the gospel and who have experience leading others to Christ. Newer residents or Christians searching for a new church home can be visited by someone from the Sunday School in their age group. An effective strategy for both types of visitation is to have a relatively large number of persons on call who can visit prospects in the area where they live—sort of a visitation "zone plan." Persons in need of counseling, on the other hand, can be visited by the pastor or other church staff.

Lewis notes that "people left on their own to visit at their convenience will seldom visit at all. For a church's visitation program to be successful, it must be organized and scheduled."[12] This is no doubt true. Survey results also show that growing churches are more likely to conduct organized visitation *more than once a week* than are plateaued and declining churches. Various strategies are possible, but the key is to provide *multiple opportunities* for prospect visitation[13] It also should be noted that the term *visitation* should be expanded to mean "going where the people are."

There are many other issues related to visitation which could be addressed. One is the number of visits necessary for each prospect. Callahan suggests that it "takes approximately five to nine visits to share effectively in mission with unchurched persons."[14] He goes on to say that efforts to do this in one or two visits are "hustling more than helping."[15] On the other hand, when prospects are Christians who are anxious to find a new church, one or two visits may be sufficient.

Another issue is whether appointments are needed before visits are made. This will vary from community to community. In general, however, the necessity of making appointments will tend to lessen the number of visits made. If visitation without appointments works, then this approach should be used. In settings where people are not generally receptive to unannounced visits or access to the building or housing development is not possible without permission, then appointments may be essential. Additionally, the visitation program of a church should be expanded to include ways of meeting people to talk about their relationships with God and with the church other than in their homes. For instance, unchurched coworkers are probably more likely to come to *your* home for dinner, than they are to accept requests by you to come to their homes in order to "talk."

A church should be flexible and use what works in its community. But the difficulty and time demands of doing prospect visitation should not be used to justify the lack of such an emphasis. When someone says, "it won't work here" do they mean "it's too much trouble" or that the traditional approach to visitation is inappropriate to this community?

Outreach is essential to the growth of most churches and prospect visitation appears to be the most effective *programmatic* emphasis which a church can organize to ensure that outreach actually occurs.

Techniques of Outreach: Revivals and Special Events

A pastor recently commented to me, "revivals don't work anymore. When I first came to this church we were having several week-long revivals each year. Now we have none, but we are still growing."

Another pastor said the opposite, "revivals are the way we get our prospects. We send notices to every address in our zip code, put signs on members lawns, and take out newspaper ads—the works. Attendance really soars during these special events, and we attract enough first-time visitors to keep our prospect visitation teams busy for months."

Are revivals, high attendance days, and other special events related to church growth? The answer is "yes," *if used properly.* Survey results show that 90 percent of growing churches have high attendance days, as compared to 83 percent of plateaued churches and 68 percent of declining churches—a definite, but not a huge relationship. Other research conducted by the Home Mission Board of the Southern Baptist Convention indicates that 24 percent of "high baptism-high growth" churches hold three or more revivals annually, as compared to only 8 percent of "high baptism-low growth" churches and 4 percent of churches in a control group composed of a cross section of SBC churches.[16] Relatively few churches have more than two revivals a year, but the incidence is *much* higher among growing congregations than it is among nongrowing congregations.

Revivals, "Friend Days," "High Attendance Sundays," "Giant Visitor's Days," "Pack a Pew Sundays," "Super Sundays," and so forth *can* result in growth, *but often do not*, because prospects are not visited quickly, and persons who join during the event may not return. Apparently, visitation and assimilation are the keys to translating a one-day surge in attendance into growth. Visits to prospects can be made *during* the revival week, as Lewis recommends, or within a few days of a high attendance Sunday, and should continue for several additional weeks and months. New members who have joined during the revival or special event should be assigned to Sunday School classes and followed up carefully. Even with these actions, attendance may drop in the weeks after the special event, but if proper efforts are made it should not decline to its previous level.

Interviews held in several churches which have grown off the plateau in dramatic fashion underscore the role special events play in "breakout growth." The pastor of a large church in Virginia which had experienced this sort of breakout growth said other churches in the area had tried to copy their Super Sunday emphases but without the same lasting results. He explained the difference in the follow up of visitors; "we visit everyone who visits us by the next week, and we keep on visiting until they either join our church or ask us not to come back."

Special events such as a singing Christmas tree, a film series, concerts by Christian musicians, a Christmas laser show, plays, Fourth of July barbecues, seminars, and the like are less likely to produce growth than are revivals or high attendance Sundays. They may serve as good publicity for the church, however, and this may produce future rewards. Regretfully, many churches do not *try* to use these events as means to secure the names of prospects. This is a mistake, because low-pressure special events may be the only way many of the true unchurched will venture near a church.

In summary, revivals and special events are related to church growth. The relationship is not as large as some might think, however, because so many churches do not use such events properly, and are thus unable to capitalize on their growth potential. Churches should examine why they hold revivals and special events. If the primary reason is "tradition," "our members enjoy them," or "to revive our church," then they are unlikely to produce growth. In fact, they may actually work against growth by siphoning off the energy of members from activities which *do produce growth.*

Techniques of Outreach: Crusades

Measuring the impact of area-wide crusades, simultaneous revivals, and other forms of mass evangelism is difficult, because there is no *good way* of determining how many baptisms and how much growth would have been recorded if the event had not been held. There is also the tendency to defend or justify the cost and effort of such events when they do not produce the desired results. People revert to the use of "war stories" about how little Suzie came to know Jesus through this crusade and that it was all worthwhile because of her; or they may say "just think of how much more baptisms would have dropped if we had not held the crusade."

There is no evidence that mass-evangelistic events help churches grow; and there is limited evidence that they actually work against growth by draining time, money, and energy from the everyday activities of local churches—which *do* produce results.

The worst examples of mass evangelism are campaigns which combine "teaser" messages with efforts to lead people to Christ over the telephone. Followup of those who make decisions is sometimes built into the process, but it rarely works. Pastors may have invested heavily in such events only to find that they did not see "one new member" as a result of participation by their church.

Some efforts at mass evangelism conducted by various Southern Baptist state conventions have tried to tie the process more closely to the local church. *Good News Texas* is one example. In 1990 a "Here's Hope" theme is being used in conjunction with nationwide simultaneous revivals and a media blitz. The jury is still out on whether such actions will make a difference in the baptism rate of the Southern Baptist Convention.

Mass evangelism sounds like a good idea, and perhaps that is why we keep doing it. It would seem to be a way of mobilizing churches to be evangelistic for a time and reaching persons who would never set foot in our churches on their own initiative. One major problem is in the area of incorporating those "reached" into the life of the church. This is a problem that Billy Graham's organization has struggled with for years, without satisfactory resolution. Another problem is that an event cannot infuse a congregation with evangelistic zeal. Doing so is a long-term process, which is necessary if a church hopes to "work their prospect list" and reach people *throughout* the year.

The most positive step that could be made in this area is to build a sophisticated evaluative research project into a major crusade or other mass evangelism event. In this way the actual results of the event could be measured. If it can be shown that churches involved in the process are more effective in reaching unchurched persons for Christ and incorporating them into the church than churches engaged in everyday evangelistic activity, then mass- evangelism efforts should be encouraged. If this is not the case, then evangelical denominations should take a hard look at curtailing crusades and simultaneous revivals.

Techniques of Outreach: Life-style Evangelism

A woman was saved through the witness of several rock musicians in a church I attended in Memphis. Practically every week thereafter, for several months, she brought friends and family members to the church whom she had already won to Christ. Eventually, all of her family were saved and most of her friends—about twenty persons in all.

Several surveys report that somewhere between two-thirds and three-fourths of church members began attending at the invitation of a family member or friend, and in growing churches the proportion tips toward friends rather than family.[17] This is not *why* these individuals joined their church, of course, but it was the reason for their *first visit.*

The question which remains is "how can life-style or network evangelism be used as a source of church growth?" After all, declining churches as well as growing churches receive visitors through these networks.

The critical factors in harnessing the growth potential within the relationship networks of church members are: (1) infusing the church with an open, evangelistic spirit; (2) having something in the church worth telling about; (3) training members in how to lead others to Christ; and (4) giving *new* Christians "permission" to share their faith with friends and family members.

Larry McSwain has said, "churches grow which are thoroughly infused with an evangelistic theology which shapes institutional structures."[18] Members must come to believe that sharing one's faith is a normal part of the Christian life. Through preaching, teaching, training, and through the examples of those around them, members may accept such a belief and make sharing their faith a part of *their* lives— even if this only means inviting someone to church, rather than actually trying to lead them to Christ. Richard Jackson reportedly began the process of building North Phoenix Baptist Church into an evangelistic congregation by asking church members on Wednesday night how many were praying by name for a lost friend or family member. Initially only a few hands were raised, but by the next Wednesday, half of those attending raised their hands. Now "approximately 80 percent of the 2,500 people who attend Wednesday night prayer meeting raise their hands saying they are praying for someone's salvation."[19]

Concerning the second key, members will not invite their friends and visitors will rarely join a church which is boring, lifeless, and cold to newcomers. For instance, a church outside Charlotte, North Carolina, languished on a plateau for years because of internal conflict, even though it had great potential for growth. Members were embarrassed to invite their friends to the church. All this changed, however, though the efforts of an interim minister who healed the wounds and through a new pastor who brought warmth and life to the church. The congregation soared of the plateau and is still growing rapidly. Members cannot restrain themselves from talking about their church and inviting their friends and neighbors to attend.

Churches also should have a group of members committed to and involved in evangelistic visitation. These members will not only invite others to attend, they will try to lead lost persons to Christ, even before they can be persuaded to visit the church for the first time. These experienced members will be active in the regular visitation program of the church and in specialized evangelistic programs, such as Evangelism Explosion or Continuing Witness Training, but they may be more effective as agents of growth through their everyday activities. As witnessing becomes a normal part of life, they will reach their friends, family members, coworkers, and casual acquaintances for Christ.

Finally, churches should not restrict evangelism and outreach to their most spiritually mature Christians. New Christians are generally more enthusiastic about their relationship with Christ than anyone else, and they have more contacts with persons who are not in the church. Further, the sudden change in the lives of new Christians gives non-Christian friends dramatic evidence of the power of God. While the impression is fresh, non-Christians can be confronted with the decision to follow the lead of their friend in accepting Christ as Savior. Pressure should not be placed on new Christians to become evangelists, however. In fact, the process usually occurs naturally, out of the new Christians's excitement about his or her relationship with Christ. All that is generally needed is the "permission" of the church to witness—even though the new believer may know little about the Bible or about "proper witnessing techniques." The expectation that all Christians should be witnesses out of the overflow of their thankfulness to God may be all that is needed to free new Christians to share their faith.

Outreach Organization

An evangelistic orientation does not develop spontaneously, or even through constant urging from the pulpit. In fact, regular preaching on witnessing shows no relationship to growth or to the number of baptisms recorded by a church. Evangelism must be built into a church and structures created to ensure that it remains an integral part of the congregation. It also must be part of the identity or guiding purpose of a congregation.

For a healthy church which has relied too heavily on biological growth, one of the best ways to begin structuring an evangelistic orientation is through a programmed growth campaign which involves evangelistic visitation. Examples of such campaigns include the Sunday School Growth Spiral, Evangelism Explosion, Growing an Evangelistic Church, and Continuing Witness Training. Evangelism must be an accepted part of the church's identity (if only at a very latent level), before such a campaign is attempted however.

As shown in figure 1.5, 67 percent of growing Southern Baptist churches participated in a programmed growth or evangelistic campaign during the past three years. By contrast, only 36 percent of plateaued churches and 35 percent of declining churches report similar participation.

Even though the various campaigns mentioned may have quite different strategies, the benefits for the church are very similar. They help institutionalize outreach activities, so outreach becomes part of the weekly church routine and part of the everyday lives of members. This is important, because the long-term benefits of *ongoing* ministries and active lay involvement tend to be far greater than the one day or one week "big push" alone. Further, having a programmed outreach plan adds to the success of one day events because trained workers are available for visitation and follow-up.

Programmed growth campaigns should not be used as a quick fixes by struggling churches, however, or by any church where such campaigns are likely to be seen as gimmicks. Instead of following the pastor's lead, the members of these churches may only wince at the thought of yet another plan to make the church grow. A campaign is a set of action

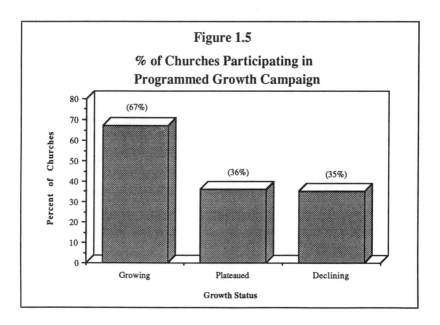

Figure 1.5

% of Churches Participating in Programmed Growth Campaign

plans designed to reach certain *goals*. And goals, of any sort, are meaningless unless they flow out of the accepted purpose or "role" of the church and are owned by the congregation.

For small struggling churches, a "pastor and allies" strategy of the type outlined by Lyle Schaller appears to be the best strategy, rather than a programmed growth campaign.[20] In this strategy the pastor preaches evangelistic messages (without berating members about not witnessing), begins to visit prospects, and recruits a few members to help with visitation. Through the personal example of the pastor, these members are then freed to share their faith. A traditional revival or high-attendance Sunday also may be planned, but with a nontraditional amount of advertising and an unusual amount of follow-up visitation.

As unchurched persons in the community are reached and as the church begins to show a little growth (or to slow its decline), the latent purpose of evangelism which most evangelical churches share may become a more salient and compelling part of the congregation's identity, and members may begin to believe that their church can break off its plateau. When this point is reached, a programmed plan for growth can be implemented to expand the number of visitors and take some of the load for outreach off the pastor.

Large, well-organized churches which are on the plateau may feel that they have already structured evangelism into the church through an evangelism committee. Unfortunately, having an evangelism committee is unrelated to church growth. Such committees sometimes exist to complete an organizational chart and do not necessarily give birth to ongoing evangelism programs. Even if a church has a minister of evangelism, as well as an evangelism committee, it should ask, "how much evangelism and outreach do we do?" If the answer is "very little other than our revivals and the visits made by the staff," then the church should rethink it approach to evangelism. Rather than assigning evangelism to a specialized subunit of the church, which is responsible for directing evangelism *for* the church, the church must infuse this task and this identity component into the life of the whole church. Specialized strategies for evangelism can then flow out of this church-wide concern for the lost without being lost from Sunday School, social ministries, recreation, worship, or other programmatic or nonprogrammatic aspects of the church.

Evangelism Training

Survey results underscore the importance of proper training for evangelism. As seen in figure 1.6, 58 percent of growing churches have a regular program for training members for evangelism, as compared to 35 percent of churches on the plateau and 26 percent of declining churches. A regular program of this sort ensures that the church has members who have the skills, motivation, and courage to visit and share their faith.

Training is especially critical for persons who have been Christians for a long time and have never made witnessing a part of their lives. A starting point should not be techniques of witnessing, however. Instead, these individuals should be led through a process where they look again at what it means to be a Christian. If nothing else, this may help provide some of the motivation, which they apparently lack.

What else should the educational process include? Programs vary, but the key to any program is training by example. James Kennedy related his experience of training members in how to witness during six-week, twelve-week, and finally fifteen-week classroom sessions—all

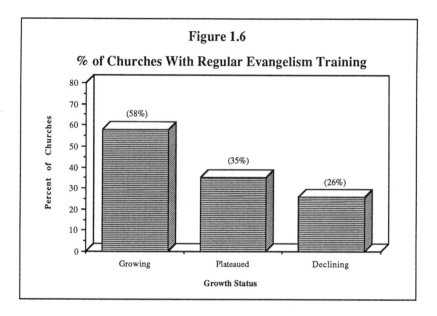

Figure 1.6

% of Churches With Regular Evangelism Training

with no results. Not one adult was brought to Christ by those trained in his witnessing classes. Then he says, "Finally it struck me like a bolt of lightning—I had taken classes for three years and had not learned how to witness. It was not until someone who knew how had taken me into people's homes that I finally got the confidence to do it myself."[21] Survey research also underscores the need for role models and "on the job training" for effective witnessing.

Witnessing is a skill which is best learned by example. It cannot be fully learned from the classroom, through books, or even through witnessing assignments. Pastors should examine their own skills and commitment in this area, as well as that of the church staff. Assigning staff to visit "x" number of prospects may produce few results if staff members have never learned how to share their faith. This is not simply a matter of learning a technique, however. Participation on a witnessing team with persons experienced in evangelistic visitation helps overcome fear, helps establish witnessing as a personal routine, helps evangelism become part of one's self-concept, and helps an individual develop a unique approach to sharing his or her experience with Christ with others.

For smaller, struggling churches evangelism training should be less programmatic. Training should be *informal* in the beginning, with the pastor taking one or two laypersons visiting, teaching them by example, and allowing them to become comfortable in witnessing to friends and other prospects.

Other Concerns

There are many other issues which could be addressed regarding evangelism and outreach. How do we avoid "sheep-stealing?" How does the need for ministry and caring fit into the activities of an evangelistic church? Should our congregation target specific populations for outreach? How can we reach the "real" unchurched in the community? How does Sunday School fit into the evangelism/outreach strategy of a church? These questions, along with others, will be covered in later chapters.

Notes

1. General Assembly Mission Council, *Membership Trends in the United Presbyterian Church in the U.S.A.* (New York: United Presbyterian Church, U.S.A., 1976), 220.

2. This yearly report by Southern Baptist churches provides extensive statistical information about churches, membership, and activities.

3. C. Kirk Hadaway, "Denominational Switching and Membership Growth: In Search of a Relationship," *Sociological Analysis* 39 (1978): 321-37.

4. Ibid. Also see C. Kirk Hadaway, "Changing Brands: Denominational Switching and Membership Change" in *Yearbook of American and Canadian Churches, 1983* (Nashville: Abingdon Press, 1983), 262-68; and Wade Clark Roof and William McKinney, *American Mainline Religion* (New Brunswick: Rutgers University Press, 1987), 148-85.

5. See C. Kirk Hadaway, "Church Growth (and Decline) in a Southern City," *Review of Religious Research* 23 (1982): 372-86.

6. Kennon Callahan, *Twelve Keys to an Effective Church* (San Francisco: Harper and Row, 1983), 11-23; Larry Lewis, *Organize to Evangelize* (Nashville: Broadman Press, 1988), 55; Lyle Schaller, *Parish Planning* (Nashville: Abingdon Press, 1971), 214; Paul W. Powell, *The Nuts and Bolts of Church Growth* (Nashville: Broadman Press, 1982), 49.

7. Clay Price, *A Study of Southern Baptist Churches with Effective Evangelistic Outreach* (Atlanta: Home Mission Board, 1985), 3.

8. Lewis, 56; Callahan, 11.

9. James Kennedy, *Evangelism Explosion* (Wheaton, Ill.: Tyndale House, 1970), 14.

10. C. Kirk Hadaway and Wade Clark Roof, "Those Who Stay Religious 'Nones' and Those Who Don't: A Research Note," *Journal for the Scientific Study of Religion* 18

(1979): 197-98. Also, James Davis and Tom W. Smith, *General Social Surveys, 1972-1989* [machine-readable data file] (Chicago: National Opinion Research Center, 1989).

11. Davis and Smith, *General Social Surveys, 1972-1989.*

12. Lewis, 60.

13. See ibid., 60-62 for a list of approaches to visitation organization.

14. Callahan, 15.

15. Ibid.

16. Price, 17.

17. Donald McGavran and George G. Hunter III, *Church Growth: Strategies That Work* (Nashville: Abingdon Press, 1980), 33-35.

18. Larry L. McSwain, "A Critical Appraisal of the Church Growth Movement," *Review and Expositor* 127 (1980): 534.

19. James Lowry, "Invitations Require Member Participation," *Facts and Trends*, November 1989, 8.

20. Lyle Schaller, *Growing Pains* (Nashville: Abingdon Press, 1984), 22-30.

21. Kennedy, 9.

2
Sunday School and Small Groups

The traditional strategy for church growth in Baptist churches, as well as for churches in many other denominations, places great emphasis on the Sunday School. Mountains of material have been published on this topic during the past fifty years, but most Baptist pastors and education directors still point to "Flake's Formula" as the key to growth through the Sunday School. According to Arthur Flake, "We must know our possibilities; enlarge the organization; provide the space; enlist and train the workers; and go after the people."[1]

Thousands of churches have used Flake's simple formula to achieve growth. Thousands of other churches have developed what they consider to be "strong Sunday Schools" and have seen growth pass them by. What is the reason for the difference? Have plateaued and declining churches deviated from Flake's formula; do they no longer work for growth; or is the true formula for growth somewhat more complex than Arthur Flake envisioned?

To address these questions it is necessary to ignore the myths and ideology surrounding the Sunday School and take a hard look at the role played by this program. Specifically, what is the purpose of Sunday School (for the church and for individual members), and how do various aspects of Sunday School organization and strategy correlate with church growth?

The Purpose of Sunday School

The central purpose of the Sunday School has never been completely clear. Some have stressed its role in outreach, while others have emphasized Bible teaching, fellowship, or new-member assimilation. In reality, Sunday School can play an effective role in all four areas, and its impact is apparently diminished when *any* are neglected.

Even though Sunday School has been called the outreach arm of the church, many churches have allowed the outreach function of the Sunday School to atrophy. When this happens the supply of new members tends to slow, existing classes stagnate, and the entire church may become a closed fellowship—existing only to serve the needs of current members.

The second function, that of Christian education, is an intended part of all Sunday Schools, but it is often taken for granted that Sunday School teaching results in *learning*. Churches tend to assume that by supplying lesson materials, teachers, and occasional training sessions that members are gaining a better understanding of the Bible and are developing a more mature Christian faith. Yet this may not be true. Some classes may have largely replaced teaching with socializing, and as Dick Murray notes, "most adult Sunday School classes try to handle too much data, too fast, in a too superficial way."[2] The object appears to be to "cover the lesson" so the class can "go on" next Sunday. As a result, the class is never able to "engage" class members with an issue or an idea which may impact their lives by challenging a preconception or adding to their understanding.[3] The focus is on the task, not on the purpose to which the task is directed.

Adding to the problem of teaching without learning is the complaint that lessons are too simplistic and that they lack substance. Difficult verses and knotty issues are often skipped, and lessons may seem somewhat obvious or bland. In reaction, some members have begun to use the services of parachurch organizations such as Precept Ministries or Bible Study Fellowship to supplement what their church provides, while others have left mainline and traditional conservative congregations to join independent Bible churches and other congregations which place a greater stress on intensive Bible study.

Unlike teaching, *fellowship* usually happens by accident rather than by design in Sunday School. In fact, it often seems that Sunday School departments are structured to see that fellowship is kept to a minimum. Rather than scheduling time for conversation, members are rushed into an opening assembly. From the assembly members are rushed to classes which end just in time for members to rush to the worship service. There is no time for fellowship, even though Sunday School provides the only structured, church-related, small-group experience for most members.

Of course, in many Sunday School classes the priorities of class members outweigh the priorities of church staff or denominational agencies. Classes may become fellowship groups in terms of their primary function, while teaching becomes accidental. Some classes may spend thirty minutes socializing and fifteen minutes on the lesson.

Pastors and church leaders should realize that it is in small groups that members develop friendship ties within the church. These relationships are *critical* to the stability of a congregation. When members have many friends in a congregation, their loyalty tends to be high, but when they have few friends, their bond to the church tends to be weak.[4] A close circle of friends also provides the sense of love and caring that people expect to find in a church. If this sense is not present, they will assume that the church is uncaring and cold, and they will continue their search for a church home elsewhere.

Finally, the role of *new member assimilation* is also neglected in Sunday School organization. New members are frequently placed in stagnant Sunday School classes with long-term members who no longer need new friendships. Sunday Schools should provide a way for new members to join groups in which they can gain rapid acceptance and develop new friends.

These are the primary functions of Sunday School. Are they all operative in your church, or do you focus on one to the neglect of others?

The Basic Relationship

Is there a strong relationship between the quality of Sunday School programming and church growth? The answer is yes. Survey questions which deal with adult Sunday School, children's Sunday School, the youth program, and singles ministry are all *strongly* correlated with church growth.

In figure 2.1 it can be seen that 84 percent of growing churches rate their adult Sunday School as *excellent or good,* as compared to only 56 percent of plateaued churches and 46 percent of declining churches. Most Southern Baptist churches have developed good Sunday School programs (or think they have). Having a good program does not *ensure* growth, but *not* having a good program will make growth extremely unlikely.

A smaller proportion of churches rate their youth programs or singles programs highly, as compared to the average rating given adult or

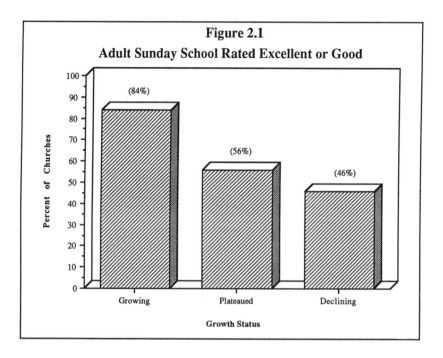

Figure 2.1

Adult Sunday School Rated Excellent or Good

children's Sunday School. However, having quality programs for youth and singles produces even stronger relationships with growth. Apparently, many churches are doing the "basics" with regard to Sunday School for adults and children, but churches (even small congregations) which go *beyond* the basics to provide quality programs for *all* groups in the church are *most likely* to experience growth.

Keeping one's youth and reaching singles are difficult tasks for most churches. An effective youth program depends to a large extent on an effective children's program for its foundation. It is as children that our members develop their values, and these values include their perception of and orientation toward the church. Vital, growing congregations give the children of members (and children who come on their own) a positive image of the church when they are young and then provide an active, meaningful youth program when they are older.

A singles ministry builds on the youth program of the church to a certain extent, but this is becoming less and less true as the average age of singles increases. Churches with successful singles ministries are reaching younger baby boomers. They are doing so with inventive programs which combine a full array of social activities with serious programs designed to meet their unique needs. When word gets around that a church has such a ministry, growth can be amazingly rapid.

A good Sunday School is not only characteristic of a growing church, the Sunday School can be used as a vehicle for helping stagnant churches grow off the plateau. Additional survey results, which can be seen in figure 2.2, show that 78 percent of breakout churches (churches which were once on the plateau but are now growing rapidly) report an "increased emphasis on the Sunday School over the past several years," as compared to 51 percent of churches which remain on the plateau. Breakout churches have improved many areas of ministry in order to grow off long-standing plateaus. Sunday School is only one of these areas, but it is apparently foundational for breakout growth.

The relationship of Sunday School to breakout growth also seems to vary by church size. For *smaller* churches the key seems to be revitalizing programs for children (for both preschoolers and school age children). For *larger* churches the key groups are singles and couples. Revitalizing Sunday School for youth is of equal importance in large and small churches.

To sum up the basic relationship, the overall quality of Sunday School programming is *very important* to church growth. Further, the direction of a church in terms of its membership trends may be altered through improvements to the Sunday School. The next question is, "what specific things make a Sunday School better, and more likely to produce growth?"

Outreach and Visitation

As was seen in the previous chapter, outreach efforts are strongly related to church growth. These efforts may be structured as a "stand alone" ministry of the church, but they are often organized and staffed through the Sunday School.

For instance, visitation frequently involves Sunday School members visiting prospects who are potential members of their own Sunday School classes. Or, the visit may be made by someone who lives nearby

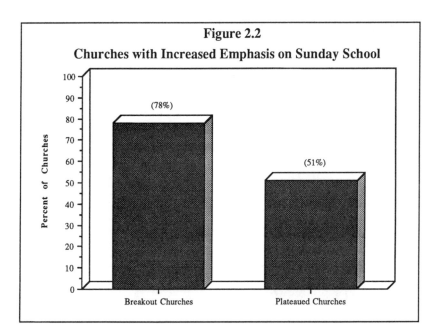

Figure 2.2

Churches with Increased Emphasis on Sunday School

the prospect. These types of contacts ensure that prospects will be visited by someone who has something in common with them, but more important it can be the beginning of a relationship between the member and the prospect. Prospects are more likely to attend Sunday School when they already know someone in the department or class to which they will be assigned or if they are accompanied to church by a neighbor.

Even for many committed Christians, the first visit to a Sunday School department in a new church produces some anxiety. Just think how a non-Christian with no church background must feel! An established relationship with a class member greatly reduces the anxiety level because visitors know they will have at least one person to talk to, as well as someone who will introduce them to others.

Survey results indicate that 55 percent of growing churches have effective Sunday School outreach programs, as compared to only 33 percent of plateaued churches and 21 percent of declining churches (see fig. 2.3). A similar relationship was found for breakout growth. A total of 56 percent of breakout churches say they have "an effective Sunday

School outreach program." Only 21 percent of churches which have continued on the plateau give a similar response.

Growing churches are clearly outreach oriented. They make a concerted effort to reach beyond themselves into the surrounding community to let others know they are welcome, wanted, and that the church has something positive to offer.

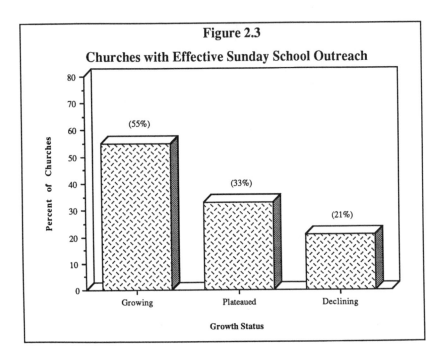

Figure 2.3

Churches with Effective Sunday School Outreach

Survey results also give insights into what growing churches are actually *doing* in the area of Sunday School outreach. For instance, a regularly scheduled time for Sunday School visitation was related to growth, as was having outreach leaders in Sunday School classes. Seventy-seven percent of growing churches have a regular time for Sunday School visitation, as compared to 53 percent of plateaued churches and 46 percent of declining churches.

This should not imply that the only visitation which is done by a church must occur during a prescribed time, one evening each week, or that outreach leaders should handle all of the Sunday School visitation.

Growing churches typically combine formal programs for visitation with informal efforts. Still, simply having outreach leaders and scheduling Sunday School visitation is significant because it indicates that the church is concerned about outreach, and it ensures that at least a *little* visitation occurs. Because of this, the presence of these things is correlated with church growth. Still, far too many churches are just filling positions or weekly schedules, rather than actually placing priority on Sunday School outreach. This leads to anemic outreach efforts, with the same small group of people showing up week after week— people who are motivated to witness in spite of the priorities of the church, rather than because of them.

All churches, and especially small stagnant churches, should place priority on outreach, and they also should put the proper *mechanisms* for outreach in place. Rarely will effective outreach develop without intentional effort by the pastor and by church leaders. Once the mechanisms are in place, continued effort must be made to see that the mechanisms are operating properly. Left unattended, they will tend to run down.

Assimilation and Retention in Sunday School and Other Small Groups

A church can operate essentially as a large *audience* for the pastor. Some churches may be able to grow with this audience character, but their growth lasts only as long as the pastor remains. Lose a great preacher and you lose the audience, unless an equally good preacher can be found quickly as a replacement.

The Sunday School and other small group settings like home cell groups, home Bible studies, choirs, missions organizations, and even committees allow a church to become *a stable web of relationships,* rather than an audience. Commitment of members is to one another, and to the whole, as well as to the pastor. Such a church is less dependent on a great preacher and is much more stable and resilient.

The church built around the Sunday School and other small groups has one problem, however, if it expects to grow. That problem is in how to maintain close bonds between members and still allow new members into the network. Preliminary research by Dan Olson on a very small number of churches has shown that in stable, nongrowing churches members have many friends and *do not feel the need for any more.*[5]

Loyalty to the congregation is very high in these churches, but newcomers cannot break into the web of relationships. In growing churches, on the other hand, members have fewer friends in the church on average and want to have more.[6]

This is one reason that newer churches tend to grow so rapidly. Members are just developing relationships with one another, and all of the social groups in the church are still permeable. Newcomers fit in easily because *everyone essentially is a newcomer.* In older churches, however, Sunday School class boundaries are often very rigid. All of the current members have known each other for years; they are comfortable with their circle of friends; and they see no real need for any more friends. They are happy to see newcomers, and may be friendly to them, but relationships are likely to remain superficial.

The church growth survey indicates that growing churches are more likely to be open and accepting of newcomers than are plateaued and declining churches. The relationship is significant, but it is not as strong as some of the correlations with church growth produced by other variables. Part of the reason for this smaller relationship is that a majority of all churches (growing, plateaued and declining) see themselves as open and accepting of newcomers.

No church wants to see itself as unfriendly and closed, and in fact, relatively few churches are obviously unfriendly. In the worst cases newcomers are simply ignored. This is not done maliciously. Members are simply more interested in socializing with their friends than in making visitors feel welcome. So after a casual, "Hi, how are you, glad to have you here," visitors are left to talk among themselves.

In most cases, however, visitors receive warm greetings but are never able to gain full acceptance into one or more of the friendship networks in the church. People are friendly to newcomers but do not become friends with them. Visitors may even join the church and attend for a few years, expecting that they will eventually develop the kind of relationships they had in their hometown churches. But it never happens, and eventually they give up hope, drop out altogether, or try again elsewhere. This type of church sees itself as friendly and accepting, but it really is not. And because so many Southern Baptist churches fit this pattern, the relationship between *self-reported* openness to newcomers and church growth is greatly reduced.

Small churches undoubtedly have a more serious problem with assimilation than do larger, "multicelled" congregations. Small churches often resemble large extended families, and to be an accepted member it is almost necessary to be born into the group or to marry a group member. Boundaries can be rigid and assimilation unlikely. It came as no surprise, therefore, that the relationship between openness to newcomers and growth was stronger among small churches than it was among larger congregations. For a small congregation to grow it *must* be open to newcomers, and, in fact, 84 percent of small growing churches said their Sunday School was "*very* open to newcomers," and 16 percent said they were "somewhat open." None of the growing churches, large or small said they were "not very open to newcomers."

For larger congregations, openness helps, but differences among growing, plateaued, and declining churches were less than was the case for small churches. The key to assimilation of new members among larger churches appears to be the presence of certain *mechanisms* which make new members feel at home and allow them to begin to develop relationships with other members of the church.

One of these mechanisms is a new member orientation class. In such classes (which should not be required) members learn about how the church operates, they find groups to join, they discover ministries in which to serve, and they can volunteer for committees in their areas of interest. New members also meet others like themselves who have few if any friends in the church, and they can begin to develop relationships with fellow newcomers.

As can be seen in figure 2.4, 76 percent of large, growing churches use new member orientation classes, as compared to 49 percent of large plateaued churches and 26 percent of large declining churches. Of course, part of the reason this relationship is so strong is that declining churches may have no need for a new member class, since they may have few new members. Still, it should be remembered that these are larger congregations which tend to have a substantial inflow of new members, but an even larger outflow.

For churches with many new members coming in, a short-term new-member class is a good idea, but for a church with few, it is probably best to assimilate these individuals into new or existing Sunday School classes.

Other strategies which help new members gain acceptance include

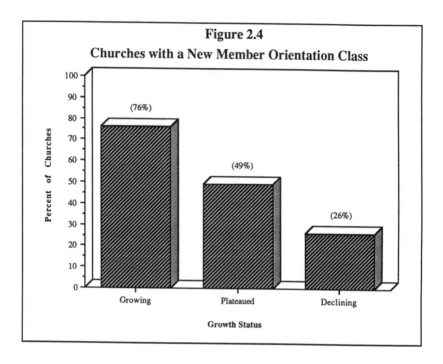

Figure 2.4
Churches with a New Member Orientation Class

the use of name tags (this only helps in large churches) and the strategy of creating new Sunday School classes for new members (both large and small churches). Name tags help new members learn the names of long-term members in large Sunday School departments. New classes for new members is a strategy which can help a church assimilate people who join as a result of evangelistic campaigns or from a high-attendance Sunday. It also allows new members to develop relationships among themselves rather than trying (often futilely) to break into established friendship networks.

Even with the best motives and the best mechanisms for assimilation, churches will always lose members "out the back door." The Sunday School can help reclaim them, but it takes good records and members who are willing to visit. Not all will return, but some will, and survey results in this area show that the effort is not wasted. A full 76 percent of churches which have experienced breakout growth report that they are exceptional or good in reclaiming lapsed members, as compared to only 45 percent of churches which remain on the plateau.

Sunday School Strategies for Growth

The Sunday School, when properly organized, is inherently designed to encourage growth and nurture. Prospects will be visited, fellowship will occur, absentees will be contacted, and needs will be shared. In short, people will be reached, assimilated, and dropouts will be kept to a minimum. With such a program operating effectively, church growth is not certain, but it is very likely.

The problem is that without proper organization, direction, and supervision the Sunday School, like the church as a whole, will tend to seek a point of least resistance—it will cease those activities which produce growth and eventually settle onto a comfortable plateau.

In order to avoid this natural tendency to plateau, strategies have been developed which are designed to reorient comfortable Sunday School programs toward outreach and to structure growth-producing characteristics into the ongoing Sunday School program. These Sunday School growth emphases help to restore the *everyday things* that a Sunday School program *should have been doing all along*. And beyond this reorientation effect, Sunday School growth campaigns also are designed to add certain organizational features which go somewhat beyond the ordinary and everyday.

At this point it should be asked, "to what extent do Sunday School growth strategies help a church to grow?" A secondary question is whether or not it is the desire and effort to achieve growth which makes the difference rather than the actual *substance* of the Sunday School growth plan.

The Importance of Enrollment

Most Sunday School growth plans put heavy emphasis on increasing Sunday School enrollment. The advice has concentrated on Sunday School enrollment, rather than on Sunday School attendance. The theory goes that attendance will tend to remain at a fixed proportion of enrollment, whether enrollment goes either up or down. Thus, a church should try to enroll as many persons as it can in Sunday School and as a result, its attendance will rise .

Does this strategy work? The answer is a guarded yes, but the link between enrollment and attendance is not *automatic*. It exists for very logical reasons, and it is these *reasons* that should be stressed, not "we don't know why it works, but it sure does work."

Survey data, combined with information from the Southern Baptist Convention's Uniform Church Letter, shows that growing churches tend to have a much higher ratio of Sunday School enrollment to resident membership than do plateaued and declining churches. In fact, as seen in figure 2.5, 51 percent of growing churches have a ratio of .9 or more, as compared to only 26 percent of plateaued churches and 19 percent of declining churches. This means that in half of the growing churches, *Sunday School enrollment is nearly equal to resident membership,* and in many growing churches, Sunday School enrollment actually *exceeds* resident membership.

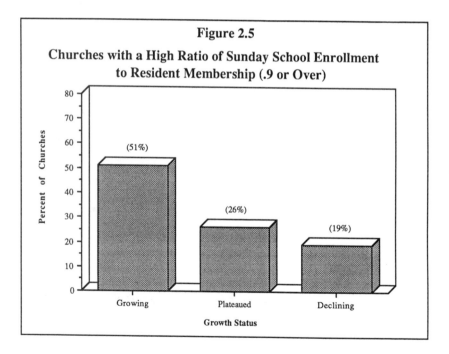

Figure 2.5

Churches with a High Ratio of Sunday School Enrollment to Resident Membership (.9 or Over)

In order to have such a high enrollment to member ratio, it is necessary for a church to place a great emphasis on enrolling large numbers of persons in their Sunday School—many of whom are not church members and may have never attended Sunday School. Enrollment of a church thus becomes a "prospect pool," which is then "worked" by active Sunday School members.

There is no secret to the relationship between enrollment and attendance. By enrolling persons we bring them under the influence of a caring small group—the Sunday School class. When such a class is accepting of newcomers and when it operates as designed, a certain percentage of uninvolved persons enrolled in Sunday School will be unable to resist the invitations and expressions of love and concern from active members. They will be drawn into the fellowship of the Sunday School class and added to the list of Sunday School *attenders*.

Increasing one's enrollment will not affect Sunday School attendance, nor the growth of the church, unless continual efforts are made to visit, invite, and involve persons who are enrolled, but who do not attend.

Multiplication or Division?

Flake's formula mentions "enlarging the organization" and modern Sunday School growth specialists speak of "multiplying units." Church members, on the other hand, call it "splitting classes." Whatever it is called, a key growth strategy for the Sunday School is to create additional classes—usually by dividing existing classes or by reorganizing the entire Sunday School according to age divisions on an annual basis.

The rationale for this strategy is that, in general, Sunday School classes tend to grow to a certain size and then stop growing. When divided into two classes, each of these "daughter" classes will also tend to grow to the same maximum size which was reached by the original "mother" class. Thus, by multiplying classes a Sunday School program will tend to grow "naturally."

The strategy of multiplying units though division has been criticized primarily because it disrupts the relationships which naturally develop in small groups. If members attend because of the love and support they gain from a network of friends developed in a Sunday School class, does it make any sense to break up the class on a regular basis? Efforts to do so also may anger class members to the point where they leave the church in order to find another which is not so callous about pursuing growth at the cost of relationships.

Dick Murray has called dividing a class "a rather bloody process of surgery,"[7] and I might add that it is old-time surgery—without anesthesia. Still, there is little doubt that the strategy works in terms of encouraging growth. Survey results show that growing churches are more likely to start new classes by dividing existing classes according to age than are plateaued or declining churches (among churches which have added classes). Growing churches are also more likely to try to divide *large* classes rather than letting them grow as big as they can.

It seems clear that Sunday School classes do tend to plateau at a level which is determined by small group dynamics. Some very large classes are possible, if the quality of the teacher is excellent, but a church will generally have few classes of this type. Churches should not necessarily discourage the existence of such classes, because there are some members who do not *want* to be in small groups and there are other members who will only attend Sunday School if a high-quality lecture is provided.

However, in order for the Sunday School as a whole to grow, new classes *must be formed*. From an organizational perspective the easiest way to do this is by *dividing* existing classes according to age. Churches which do not like this strategy are faced with the problem of finding alternative means of starting classes. Too often they take the easier route and leave their Sunday School classes alone. The result is a plateau for these classes, which eventually causes the Sunday School to plateau, which in turn may cause the entire church to stop growing.

Churches which are committed to growth and which do not like the idea of splitting classes may use other strategies such as beginning new classes "from scratch" with a few "seed" members recruited from other classes, by recruiting persons presently inactive in Sunday School to form new classes, or by instituting a university-style Sunday School in which *no* ongoing classes exist.

Growing churches have used each of these alternative strategies, but it should be noted that the alternatives are much more difficult the traditional "Baptist way." Further, a church which pursues a nontraditional strategy faces a greater possibility of settling into the still easier route of not beginning *any new classes*. This will eventually result in an attendance plateau. Even worse, the church which pursues the university-style program may face the possibility of *severe declines* in attendance if program oversight is neglected. The sad story of adult Sunday

School attendance *evaporation* in thousands of mainline churches can be used as evidence to support this argument.

In order to maximize growth through the Sunday School, a church must start new classes. The easiest way to do this is by splitting classes along age lines. Unfortunately, this also creates problems which *may hurt growth.* To deal with this problem a church can either: (1) stress the importance of creating new units from the pulpit, so that members are "sold" on the need; or (2) use another strategy to create new units, but work very hard to see that new units actually are developed.

Other Emphases

(A) High attendance days.—Special days such as high attendance days, friend days, and the like are related to church growth. They work for three reasons. First, if efforts are made to contact Sunday School members who have not attended in a while, it may be possible to "reactivate" a certain proportion of lapsed members. Second, if the Sunday School enrollment roster includes a large number of prospects (as it should), a special event may be the thing which provokes them to attend for the first time. Third, if efforts are made to attract new people from the community, the church *may* gain new members who are impressed by the vitality apparent in the larger-than-usual church family, and it *will* gain an entirely new set of prospects which can be contacted over the next few months. On the other hand, if no real effort is made to promote the special event and if it is only used to get regular attenders to all show up on one day, then the event will not produce any lasting growth. In fact, the next Sunday may see a record low attendance.

(B) Setting class enrollment goals.—Churchwide membership goals often have the same limitations as the goals set by the denomination—they are not owned (or even recognized) by the folks who must do the work in order for the goals to be reached. Allowing individual Sunday School departments or classes to set their own goals makes these units aware of their attendance and enrollment patterns and gets them involved in trying to grow. It helps to have something to shoot for, and most Sunday School classes are not concerned about how their class fits into the overall growth strategy of the church. They are concerned with the mechanical operation of the class, the quality of the teaching, the satisfaction of those who come, and whether or not they have a good

crowd. Growth goals reorient the priorities of the class, so that prospects and outreach become more than"things Sunday School classes are supposed to do."

(C) Pastor's class.—Having a pastor's class *is* related to growth, but the relationship is relatively weak except in larger churches. In smaller churches, where few adult classes exist, a pastor's class may undermine the health of the other classes to the point where the church has only one large class for couples—taught by the pastor. Such a class may grow, but it will hurt the chances of long-term growth for the Sunday School program as a whole. It also makes recruiting teachers and students for alternative adult classes all the more difficult.

For large churches, a pastor's class is less likely to cause problems for the Sunday School program because many adult classes already exist and most members are already committed to their own Sunday School classes. The pastor's class provides a comfortable large-group setting for those who are uneasy in small groups, for those who insist on a lesson which is professional and polished, and for marginal members who want a low-commitment taste of Sunday School before they take a full bite. Such a class helps a church provide "something for everyone," and as such, it helps the larger church grow. However, such classes may also *prevent* shy members from ever becoming fully integrated into the life of the church. In a large lecture forum they may never get to know other class members and remain essentially unassimilated, solitary members, without the "redundant ties" to various small groups which ensure commitment and stability.[9] Some mechanism should be in place to encourage persons who attend the pastor's class to "graduate" into other Sunday School classes.

Organization and Training

An effective Sunday School program requires proper organization—it will not run by itself. Curriculum must be selected, teachers and department leaders recruited, vacancies filled, visitation organized, classes graded, new classes started, records kept and evaluated, goals set, special emphases coordinated, and a host of other organizational tasks conducted.

Large churches, whether growing or not, tend to have the basic organization in place, with oversight by a full-time minister of education. The *difference* between growing and non-growing churches is in *how well the machinery runs and whether or not the model is "stripped" or "fully loaded."* Teacher training, for instance, is related to church growth among larger congregations, but the relationship is only moderate in strength. This is due to the fact that nearly all larger churches do some kind of teacher training. On the other hand, weekly workers meetings produce a much stronger correlation with growth. Most plateaued and declining churches tend to skip this program, while over three quarters of growing churches hold weekly workers' meetings. A similar pattern was seen for the use of name tags in *larger churches.* Only 9 percent of plateaued churches and 2 percent of declining churches used name tags in Sunday School, as compared to a full 28 percent of larger growing churches.

Large *growing* churches do the basics—and then some. They add options here and there to "tweak" maximum performance out of the Sunday School program. By contrast, larger plateaued and declining churches tend to only include the basics, and some of these churches have even let the basics slide. Apparently they have allowed their Sunday Schools to regress toward the "path of least resistance." To complete the "vehicle" analogy, they have shifted into neutral; and while this allows most to idle on a plateau, churches located in older urban neighborhoods or stagnant rural villages have started to roll backwards.

Smaller churches tend to be less organized than do larger congregations. However, small growing churches tend to have a Sunday School organization which resembles larger churches rather than onewhich resembles other small congregations. This pattern, which also was found for breakout churches (churches which had grown off the plateau), seems to indicate that in order to grow, or to ensure that growth continues, smaller growing churches have tried to emulate the organizational structure and activities of larger congregations. They have started training *new* Sunday School teachers and hold some kind of teacher training for *all* teachers during the year. Some even have added weekly workers' meetings. Apparently acting like you are large helps a church begin to grow in that direction. On the other hand, because these churches are still relatively small, they see no need for things like name tags. Everyone still knows one another and suggesting that the class use name tags may imply that it is no longer a "family."

For this reason, small growing churches are slightly *less* likely to use name tags than are small declining churches.

Also related to training is the *seriousness* with which a church approaches Christian education. Most churches see Christian education as a natural result of a good Sunday School program. Teachers are recruited, they are given lesson materials, and they are encouraged to attend a weekly meeting to discuss approaches to Sunday's lesson. That's about it. The church assumes that teachers are knowledgeable, competent, and performing well in their role as Sunday School teachers. For a few churches, however, this approach takes too much for granted and they have taken additional steps to ensure that students are learning biblical truth and ways to apply these truths to everyday life.

In First Chinese Southern Baptist Church in Los Angeles, and in a small number of other Southern Baptist churches, teacher training is a very serious business, and it may take a year or more before new teachers are allowed to have classes of their own. Teachers must have a basic knowledge of the Bible and theology, know how to interpret the Bible, know how to communicate biblical truths, and have an understanding of the characteristics of the age group which they will teach. These skills only allow a person to become an intern teacher, however. After a successful year in this role, the intern may take the job of associate teacher working with a lead teacher, and eventually may become a lead teacher. This lengthy process, which may seem excessive and impractical for churches which have a very difficult time recruiting workers, is deemed necessary because of the importance attached to Christian education at First Chinese Baptist Church. The congregation is determined to see that members mature in the Christian faith and these steps ensure that it happens.

Churches which are this serious about Christian education tend to grow, but to develop a system of training so elaborate takes time. It may not even be feasible for most Southern Baptist churches. Still, nearly all churches can stand vast improvements in their efforts in teacher training and preparation.

Other Small Groups

Sunday School is not the only small-group experience for many church members. Others groups include the choir, committees, mission organizations, task forces, training groups, and various forms of home Bible studies or cell groups. Each of these groups adds to the number of face-to-face contacts a member has in the church and increases his or her circle of friends. The groups help create a large number of redundant ties which bind an individual to a church.[10] The more ties exist, the stronger is the bond.

Home cell groups, home Bible studies, care and share groups, and the like are becoming an increasingly important source of small-group experience—in some cases rivaling Sunday School in importance and attention. A few churches even have half-time or full-time directors of their home-cell ministries. In many cases the model for the development of such a ministry has been Yoido Full Gospel Church in Seoul, Korea. This congregation has used a home-cell strategy to become the largest church in the world with 600,000 members. Other than growth, a further impetus for home-cell ministries has been the realization that in most Sunday School classes and other small groups, fellowship, nurture, and mutual support in times of need happens largely by accident. In home cell groups, by contrast, this sort of *koinonia* and the development of strong caring relationships are "built in."

Southern Baptist churches in the United States have been relatively slow to adopt home cell groups, at least in comparison to their rapid acceptance by charismatic churches, independent churches, and by Baptist congregations in England and on the mission field. Even so, survey data shows that having a home-cell ministry is related to church growth among Southern Baptist churches. The relationship is not strong, but then most Southern Baptist churches which have home-cell groups only seem to be testing the water, others have experienced problems with the ministry conflicting with the Sunday School program, and still other churches have not organized the cell groups with growth in mind.

The need for cell groups seem clear—they provide a function for members which is being neglected by most churches. Because of this useful function, home cell groups do help churches grow. It remains to be seen, however, whether or not home-cell groups will become a major ministry for Southern Baptist churches. If they do not, church leaders should be aware of the extent to which the needs for nurture, fellowship, and mutual support are being met by existing church programs. If these needs are not being met and if members are dissatisfied because of the situation, they may leave Southern Baptist churches for congregations which emphasize nurture and fellowship, or they may turn to parachurch groups for small group support.

Things That Don't Work as Advertised

Room to grow.—Growing churches tend to be out or nearly out of educational space. Plateaued and declining churches, by contrast, tend to have lots of room. This makes sense. Growing churches have filled up their educational space through their growth and are now bursting at the seams. The question is whether or not their growth will now continue—since they are running out of space for new Sunday School classrooms and most of their existing classes are full.

It is possible for a church to begin to plateau because it is out of educational space, but this is not a major reason why so many Southern Baptist churches are on statistical plateaus. The vast majority have plenty of room to grow.

It would appear that growing churches tend to fill up their educational space rather rapidly. This "fullness" does create problems, of course. Smaller departments with excess space may be asked to switch rooms with rapidly growing departments. Space that is not meant for housing Sunday School classes may have to be commandeered for this purpose, and churches even may be forced to follow the example of overcrowded schools and use temporary buildings and trailers. While this situation taxes the creativity of the Sunday School director or minister of education, it also creates the exciting sense that "something is happening here." For this reason, being full may tend to encourage growth rather than discourage it.

There is a limit, however, to the number of new people an already full Sunday School can absorb. Plans should be made to build additional education space or to go to multiple Sunday Schools before growth levels off. New space is costly, takes time to construct, and land may not be available. Multiple Sunday Schools are much less costly, but beginning an additional Sunday School is a gut-wrenching process which requires a complete reorganization of all classes, recruiting many new teachers, tremendous promotion efforts, and altering the set Sunday schedules of most active members.

A church should never try to build as much space as "we will ever need," because the transition from overcrowded conditions to "more than enough room" produces too much change in what social psychologists call the "psycho-spatial dynamics." The exciting crowded feeling that "something is happening here" may be replaced by the awkward feeling of too few people in too large a room. Members may even assume that the Sunday School is declining because it no longer feels crowded.

From a church growth perspective it would be best to build just ahead of one's growth. And, in fact, this is what many growing churches do—although unintentionally. New space is often comfortably filled as soon as completed, and within a year or two the Sunday School may be overcrowded again. This situation, while inconvenient, is a problem that thousands of churches would like to have.

Small classes.—Growing churches tend to have *larger* Sunday School classes than do plateaued or declining churches. This is true even though growing churches make an effort to divide large classes and tend to start new classes by splitting existing classes according to age.

It would appear that small classes do not tend to encourage growth *simply because they are small.* In fact, most plateaued and declining churches have small classes and plenty of educational space. Growth comes for other reasons, and churches which have these growth-producing factors in place must fight to keep their classes at a reasonable size.

Many people think that simply splitting classes will encourage growth. They split their classes, add new teachers, and wait for growth to hit them. Frequently the reverse occurs. The process disrupts existing friendship networks, so that members become less excited about attending. Very small classes which lack close relationships among the members attending can kill discussion and create long periods of embarrassing silence when the teacher invites the class to talk. Further, small classes may drive away first-time visitors who find themselves in a class with only the teacher and one or two other members.

When classes become too large for the room or when discussion is beginning to suffer in growing churches, efforts should be made to divide a growing class using the techniques discussed earlier. This will allow growth to continue. Plateaued churches, on the other hand, should not simply split classes in order to get class sizes down to recommended levels. Any effort to "multiply units" should be coupled with procedures to make the Sunday School more attractive to newcomers, more willing to accept them, and more aggressive about inviting them to attend.

Bus ministry.—The bus ministry is a traditional technique for producing rapid growth in Sunday School, especially when the target has been children in working-class or lower middle-class neighborhoods. Some churches apparently are still able to use bus ministries as "vehicles" for growth, but it is clear that the golden age of the bus ministry is long past.

Survey results show that only a small minority of Southern Baptist churches growing churches use bus ministries, and growing churches are no more likely to use them than are plateaued and declining churches. The possible reasons for this finding are varied. The growth which results from a bus ministry is often fleeting. Children may be attracted but it is difficult to reach their parents, or it may be that the technique simply may be less successful today than it was in the 1950s. Whatever the reason, most churches would be ill-advised to attempt a major bus ministry in order to achieve growth. The effort is very likely to fail. Nevertheless, churches should provide transportation for members and prospects who can't get to church easily on their own. This may imply the need for a bus ministry of some sort, but not of the type which was prevalent in the 1950s and 1960s.

A Final Word About Sunday School

This chapter, although lengthy, has only scratched the surface of how Sunday School and other small groups impact the growth of churches. Books have been written on the subject, and the reader is directed to them if further information is needed on the "nuts and bolts" of using the Sunday School to help your church grow. I have tried to cover the major issues and to deal with some of the more glaring myths surrounding the Sunday School.

While the conclusions drawn in this chapter have no corner on truth, they are based on "real data" rather than speculation or unsystematic observation. As such, the reader would be wise to use them in order to "reality test" the more specific growth suggestions and growth strategies found elsewhere.

Notes

1. Arthur Flake, as quoted by Paul Powell in *The Nuts and Bolts of Church Growth* (Nashville: Broadman Press, 1982), 67-68.

2. Dick Murray, *Strengthening the Adult Sunday School Class* (Nashville: Abingdon Press, 1981), 87.

3. Ibid., 87-89.

4. Daniel V. A. Olson, "Church Friendships: Boon or Barrier to Church Growth?," *Journal for the Scientific Study of Religion* 28 (1989): 432-47.

5. Ibid., 442.

6. Ibid., 443.

7. Murray, 50.

8. Ibid., 45.

9. Lyle E. Schaller, "Redundant Ties," *The Parish Paper* 17 (1987): 1.

10. Ibid.

3
Worship and Church Growth

Worship in growing churches, and especially in rapidly growing churches, has a different character from worship in plateaued and declining congregations. This character is somewhat difficult to describe, but the terms usually employed are "excitement," "celebration," "electricity," and "spirit of revival." Whatever terms are used, anyone who has worshiped in many growing congregations will agree that the worship experience sets these churches apart.

Bryant Wright, who is pastor of a large, innovative, and rapidly growing congregation north of Atlanta, visited thirty six well-known, growing churches across the United States. He relates that "there was an excitement in the air—people were eager to get inside to worship and to fellowship with one another." It was an atmosphere which he could only describe as similar to "the crowd that gathers before a big sporting event . . . this is the place to be at this hour."[1] In a similar fashion, Peter Wagner says, "when a lot of people come together, hungry to meet God, a *special* kind of worship experience can occur. That experience is what I want to call 'celebration.' "[2] Medford Jones adds to the list of adjectives describing worship in growing churches, "a spirit of freedom, spontaneity, and even exuberance."[3]

For pastors of nongrowing churches or even churches which are growing, the above descriptions may not seem to be very helpful as they try to move their churches toward growth or ensure that growth continues. The pastors of many nongrowing churches may realize that worship in their church is anything but a "celebration," but they do not know how it can *become* a celebration. Conversely, the pastors of growing churches may know that there is something special about worship in their church, but they may not understand how it got that way or how to restore the special spirit when the "celebration" begins to turn into a wake.

This chapter will explore the setting, content, and spirit of the worship service in order to help pastors and other church leaders understand exactly what it is about worship in growing churches which is different; and how nongrowing churches can begin to infuse some "life" into the worship experience of their own congregations.

The Setting for Worship

Exciting worship can occur in all types of churches, but apparently it is encouraged by the presence (or appearance) of a *crowd*. Despite the rule of thumb that a worship service in which more than 80 percent of the seats are filled *is too full*, such is the norm among large growing churches. In fact, in a survey of growing, plateaued, and declining Southern Baptist churches, it was found that the worship services in slightly over 80 percent of the growing churches with large total memberships (over 485 resident and nonresident members) were more than 80 percent full. According to Lyle Schaller, "there is no question but that when all the pews or chairs are filled, this has a positive impact on the morale of the worshipers, and especially on the preacher."[4] The appearance of a crowd creates the sense that "something is happening here." Morale is higher, as Schaller says, and it is easier to create the feeling of a "festival" or "celebration."

The worship services in small *growing* churches are more likely to be filled than are those in plateaued and declining churches of a similar size. However, only about half of the small growing churches are over 80 percent filled (as compared to the much larger percentage of large growing churches which are this full). The intimate environment of a small church and the natural close proximity of those worshiping together means that a small church can create the exciting feeling of a crowd even when it is only half filled.

For a large church, the exciting feeling of a crowd only comes when the church is full or nearly full. When a large church is half empty, persons are scattered around the sanctuary with large spaces between them. The first five or six rows are empty. Participants do not interact much with one another. They sit and wait for the "show."

The impact of a crowd is never more evident than when a congregation moves into a much larger worship facility. I attended a church in

Memphis which was filled to overflowing on Sunday morning and Sunday evening. The services were exciting, celebrative, and enthusiastic—but it was hard to get a seat. The church relocated, and for a while met in a temporary auditorium. This changed the dynamics somewhat, but the real shock was the first Sunday in the completed sanctuary. The worship service went from standing room only in the old auditorium to no more than 30 percent full in the new setting, even though the balcony was roped off for "future growth." In a single week the crowded feeling was gone, the excitement was gone, the sense of a "festival" was gone. And morale dropped as well. Attendance had not changed in that week, but the church looked like it was dying. The perception of problems soon turned into reality. The church stopped growing, lost many of its younger members, and fifteen years later sold its huge facility and relocated to a smaller building. Overbuilding was not the only problem of this congregation, of course, but it certainly was one of several which together caused it to stop growing.

Large growing churches face a dilemma. A church which is 80 percent full has little room for future growth, yet it cannot afford to lose the dynamic which occurs when large numbers of excited Christians worship together in a crowded sanctuary. *This spirit feeds the growth of the church.* Not only do visitors feel excited and impressed, but a larger proportion of resident members will regularly attend. As Wright observed, "this is the place to be" and members will not miss the experience if they are in town.[5]

The lesson here is that churches should never overbuild to accommodate growth for the next five or ten years. Instead, they should go to multiple services prior to new construction, and then build when these services are filled. The new sanctuary probably should be no less than 65 to 70 percent filled when the services are consolidated.

For larger churches which are not filled, efforts should be made to make the worship service *seem* filled—"forcing" members to sit closer to one another and removing the impression of a few people rattling around in a large room. Rows of pews can be removed from the front and rear, or the pulpit can be moved forward. Other changes may be possible. This may not immediately create a spirit of celebration, but if a church can *begin* to grow through other means, the worship experience can be transformed from a liability into an asset. As the church grows, and as members sit closer together, a new dynamic may be created which enables the church to grow *even faster*.

Another feature regarding the setting for worship, other than size and fullness, is the *appearance* of the sanctuary or auditorium. Common sense would suggest that churches should be kept in good repair—and all should be. Yet is is easy to overlook the peeling paint, water spots, stained carpet, missing light bulbs, and so forth. Just as we get accustomed to the flaws in our own homes, church members get used to flaws in the church—so much so that they do not even notice them. But *visitors do notice the flaws*, and too many flaws give the impression that the church is having financial problems or that the members just don't care.

Appearance is less of a problem for small rural churches or for churches in older urban neighborhoods. In fact, in such settings there is no relationship between the "need for work" on the sanctuary and church growth. For large churches the situation is entirely different. They cannot get away with shabby sanctuaries. Large, growing churches tend to be in good repair. It is also true that larger churches which have grown off the plateau tend to have worship facilities which are in better repair than churches which remain on the plateau. Thus, it would appear that the symbolic step of renovating, restoring, painting, or just fixing long-standing flaws can be of value in restoring morale and creating the impression that the plateaued church is about to get moving again.

The Content of Worship

A worship service is a dynamic mix of congregational singing, prayer, choir anthems, announcements, ritual, testimony, liturgy, solos, instrumentals, organ music, a sermon, an offering, Scripture reading, sitting, standing, and interacting with persons seated nearby. Some churches may add to this mix other elements such as a children's sermon, drama, clapping and swaying to the music, "passing the peace," a processional, a recessional, and so forth. The nature of this content, and its *quality* affects the character of worship in terms of meaning, enjoyment, boredom, excitement, morale, and whether one feels they have encountered God in the experience.

There is no central core of worship elements or a particular style which characterizes all growing churches. As Wright concluded after his visits to many congregations, "the styles of worship varied greatly; there simply is no set formula. Some were very formal and structured; some were very free."[6] Still, research shows that certain styles of worship may be somewhat more conducive to church growth than others.

Liturgy

The presence of "liturgy" is more characteristic of churches on the plateau than it is of growing churches (or of declining churches) *in the Southern Baptist Convention.* Plateaued churches are also much more formal, on average, than are declining churches or *growing churches.* Growing churches are less likely to have liturgy and are less formal on average than *declining churches,* but the major difference is between plateaued churches and churches which are not on the plateau.

Liturgical Southern Baptist churches tend to be stable, staid, and upper-middle class. Their worship may be very meaningful, but it does not tend to have the quality of celebration or revival spirit which is so characteristic of growing churches. Liturgy in Baptist churches is like caviar. One must learn to like it, and only upper-class Baptists have the inclination to do so. There are so few of such individuals available that most liturgical Southern Baptist churches are unable to grow.

For churches which are on the plateau that wish to grow, research clearly shows that formality and liturgy are often barriers. These churches need excitement and life, and is it hard (though not impossible) to wed formality and excitement. For this reason, Southern Baptist churches which have grown off the plateau tend to be considerably less formal and liturgical than churches which remain on the plateau.

In denominational traditions where liturgy and formality are the norm, it is not the presence of these elements which tends to restrict growth, but how they are done. Liturgical worship can be very meaningful and, in fact, it may help create a greater sense of spirituality and of an encounter with a living God, than does the traditional task-oriented conservative Protestant worship service. Unfortunately, in too many mainline and Catholic churches, the services tend to produce boredom rather than meaning.

The Sermon

Although the pastor's sermon is a frequent topic of conversation among church members, there is not as much correlation between church growth and the quality (and style) of preaching as might be expected. For instance, the relationship between being a "dynamic preacher" and church growth was found to be statistically significant among Southern Baptist churches, but it was quite weak in strength. The relationship between preaching "exciting" sermons and church growth is stronger, but not nearly as strong as that produced by the rating given music and choirs, for instance.

Some pastors may be able to cause a church to grow by the sheer force of their excellence as preachers. Such pastors are few and far between, however, and for the bulk of churches, the objective "quality" of sermons has relatively little to do with growth. More important is the centrality of the Bible in sermons, being able to generate enthusiasm in worship, the communication of a vision for the future of the church, and maintaining high morale. Which is more important? That is highly debatable, but Doug Murren, pastor of a rapidly growing Foursquare church in Washington says, "spiritual climate control is my number one role as the pastor of my church."[7] In other words, enthusiasm and high morale create the climate necessary for leadership to operate and for the message of sermons to be heard.

Music

Warren Hartman and Robert Wilson, in their study of large Methodist churches, indicate that music is more important for the members of larger churches than it is for mid-sized and small churches.[8] My research indicates, however, that while the music tends to be objectively *better* in large churches, the *relationship* between church and the quality of music in worship is quite strong in both large and small Southern Baptist churches.

Figure 3.1 shows the relationship between church growth and the rating of the music ministry and choirs. A full *90 percent* of large, growing churches rate their music program as excellent or good, as compared to 78 percent of plateaued churches and 53 percent of declining churches. Among smaller churches, 65 percent of growing congregations rate their music program as excellent or good, as compared to 37 percent of plateaued churches and 35 percent of declining churches. Obviously, a strong relationship exists for large *and* small churches.

Music makes a difference to the growth of a church; so pastors, worship leaders, choir directors or ministers of music should take planning

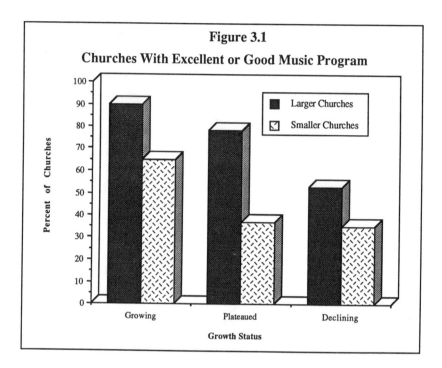

Figure 3.1

Churches With Excellent or Good Music Program

music very seriously. Too many churches have piano players who are too old to hit all the notes; too many churches have choirs which have not practiced, cannot carry a tune, or have not been trained to sing in harmony; and too many churches sing and play a single type of music which may fit a large segment of the congregation, but which does not interest unchurched residents in the community.

Kennon Callahan says "a strong music program has three ingredients: planning and spontaneity, balance and variety, and quality and depth."[9] Music should be carefully planned, but with a certain amount of spontaneity built in. A few unplanned choruses after a hymn will not wreck the service, and they may create a feeling of spontaneity and life. Not all members have the same musical tastes, and not all music provokes the same feeling among members. The music should be inoffensive to all and chosen to follow the theme or mood of the service, but it should also have enough variety so that all members and all visitors will hear something which they enjoy. Eighteenth-century hymns can be mixed with Bach concertos, classical guitar solos, gospel choruses, Negro Spirituals, and contemporary Christian gospel. How can the worship leader or choir director find out what the people in the church and in the community want and what might offend them? They can be asked, and then the proper mixture created.

A church should be especially sensitive to the musical tastes of the unchurched in their community. In rural areas, a church might find that local residents enjoy traditional hymns, but if a suburban church wishes to reach the baby boom generation, it would do well to add a healthy dose of tasteful contemporary Christian gospel along with more traditional church music. Before condemning such music because of its beat, church leaders should listen to the words and ask themselves how serious are they about reaching the lost. Do we only want members who grew up in Protestant churches and who only like eighteenth-century hymns? If so, then we will have to rely on the many independent churches, which are less bound by tradition, to reach large numbers of baby boomers who were raised on rock and roll.

One gauge of success is whether or not the music "stirred one's heart," to use Wright's words.[10] If it does so for both members and visitors, then music will likely help your church to grow. If it does not, then change should be made to add spontaneity, balance, variety, quality, and depth in what ever quantities your church lacks.

To gain some perspective on what you church lacks, an excellent strategy is to visit the worship services of growing churches of your denomination and other churches of *various traditions* which are known for their exciting and uplifting worship. In Washington, D. C., for instance, the services of Saint Augustine Catholic Church should not be missed. Although the use of drums, saxophone, trumpet, flute, and tambourine may be unfamiliar to many white Protestants, no one can come away from their worship services unmoved. If nothing else, a soloist backed up by a swaying, clapping choir, singing Jesus on the cross "would *not* come down—He *decided* to die—to set me free" would be enough to touch most people in the service.

Other Elements of Worship

Some elements of worship cannot be considered sources of growth, and if done badly they can detract from the overall worship experience and work against growth. *Announcements* are normally boring, so they should be kept short and be read by someone who can give them a little life. *Prayers* and *Bible reading* can also be boring, if done poorly or without apparent meaning. Some people are recognized "prayer warriors" who constantly intercede in prayer for their friends and who see results. Why not use them to pray, rather than rotating the responsibility among a large number of members? Similarly, some Christians read well and others read poorly, while still others are able to give the impression that they are reading the most important words that have ever been written. A church in Los Angeles used a professional actor who changed his voice to fit the biblical character who was speaking to read Scripture. Are there members of your church who are involved in radio or television, or who simply have powerful reading voices. Why not use them to do the Scripture reading? Alternatively, why not use persons to read who are able to convey a great sense of feeling and meaning to what they read?

Dead spots should be eliminated whenever possible, such as allowing speakers or readers to walk back to their chair before the next action occurs. *Testimonies* can add life and a spiritual dimension to a lifeless worship service. A church in Norfolk, Virginia, has evangelistic visitation on Sunday afternoon because it found that most people are home at that time. This schedule allows testimonies in the Sunday evening worship service from persons who have seen lost persons saved *that* afternoon. What dramatic evidence that God is at work through the members of the church! Similarly, a church in rural Arkansas performs all of its baptisms on Sunday morning so that a larger proportion of the membership can see that people are being saved through the witness of church members.

The Spirit of Worship

Among survey questions which dealt with worship, those tapping the "spirit" or "mood of worship" produced the strongest correlations with church growth. To put it simply, growing churches tend to have worship services which are *joyful, expectant, celebrative,* and which have a *spirit of revival.* Not only are all of these characteristics related to church growth, but they also tend to go together. That is, the church where worship has a sense of expectancy also tends to have a spirit of revival.

Of all the characteristics used to measure the spirit of worship in

Southern Baptist churches, the strongest relationship with growth was produced by the "spirit of revival" question. As can be seen in figure 3.2, 60 percent of growing churches reported that they always or usually have a spirit of revival in worship, as compared to only 26 percent of plateaued churches and 22 percent of declining churches. Like evangelism, this characteristic seems to be an all or nothing affair. Growing churches tend to have it, while nongrowing churches (plateaued or declining) do not.

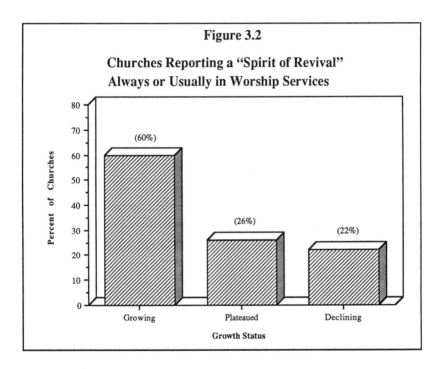

Figure 3.2

Churches Reporting a "Spirit of Revival"
Always or Usually in Worship Services

Additional characteristics of worship in growing churches are a sense of warmth, spontaneity, enthusiasm, and variety. People express love and welcome to one another; the order of service leaves room for alteration if the Spirit moves; members are enthusiastic rather than somber in their worship; and the church does not do the same thing week after week. Different styles of music are employed, the order of worship is varied, special theme services are used, tradition and innovation are alternated or even intermingled.

According to Kent Hunter, "worship should be a celebration." But there also are things it should not be if the church expects to grow. Hunter goes on to say worship "is not intended to be a dull, drab, funeral atmosphere."[11] Peter Wagner adds that there is nothing unauthentic about boring worship but if it is boring, members will not be very enthusiastic about inviting unsaved friends.[12] Research data on Southern Baptist churches tends to support these generalizations. *Plateaued* and *declining* churches are more likely to say their worship sometimes (or frequently) is characterized by *monotony, boredom,* and *formality.*

Worship services can be fun and exciting experiences, but too often they are not. Too much formality, a task-oriented sense that the purpose of worship is to get through the order of service, and worship planning which is unresponsive to the needs and preferences of members results in worship that is boring and monotonous. Church members attend such services for a variety of reasons, but one of these reasons is not that they like to be bored. They go *in spite* of being bored. For unchurched persons who have relatively little motivation to attend church in the first place, a boring and overly predictable service only serves to reinforce the reasons that they left the church.[13]

Growing churches are primarily those churches which are being successful in attracting the thirty- to forty-five year old baby boom generation. Why? This is the largest age segment of the population in its own right, and it also is the age segment most likely to have children in the home. Add the boomers and their children together and you have a huge group of people—a large proportion of whom have either dropped out of the church or have adopted a "mental member" status, where they identify with the church but rarely attend. Churches which are able to reach this group will grow because middle age and older persons are *already in the churches*, and young single adults are even more difficult to reach than are the baby boomers.

The thirty to forty-five age group is so important that churches have emerged which focus their efforts on reaching this population alone. Churches like Willow Creek Community Church in South Barrington, Illinois, are unapologetic about reaching the baby boom generation. Using Christian rock music, drama, multimedia slide shows, along with more traditional worship features, the church is trying to reach persons whom the pastor calls "unchurched Harrys"—persons who see the church as irrelevant, stodgy, boring, and predictable. To do this the church makes sure that it is anything but irrelevant, stodgy, and boring. In the words of Bill Hybels, the pastor, "this is the generation that grew up on television . . . you have to present religion to them in a creative and visual way."[14] For this population, to be boring is the worst characteristic of all.

This does not mean that *all* churches should emulate the worship style of Willow Creek Community Church. But it does mean that mainline and conservative denominations should have churches targeting the unchurched baby boomer population in major cities across the United States. Such churches could learn much from Willow Creek Community Church or from Saddle Back Valley Community Church about which traditional aspects of worship to keep and which to lose. For most churches, however, the focus should be on adding variety, sound planning, spontaneity, expectation, excitement, celebration, warmth, and quality music to their worship services.

Notes

1. Bryant Wright, "Observations on Church Growth," *The Christian Index*, August 24, 1989, 8.

2. C. Peter Wagner, *Your Church Can Grow*, rev. ed. (Ventura, Calif.: Regal Books, 1984), 111.

3. Medford H. Jones, "Dynamic Churches Come in All Sizes," in *Church Growth: State of the Art*, eds. C. Peter Wagner, Win Arn, and Elmer Towns (Wheaton, Ill.: Tyndale House, 1986), 137.

4. Lyle E. Schaller, "One Worship Service or Two?" *The Parish Paper* 9 (1980):1.

5. Wright, 8.

6. Ibid.

7. Doug Murren, "Congregational Climate Control," *Ministries Today*, July-August 1989, 32.

8. Warren Hartman and Robert Wilson, *The Large Membership Church* (Nashville: Discipleship Resources, 1989), 18.

9. Kennon Callahan, *Twelve Keys to an Effective Church* (New York: Harper and Row, 1983), 27.

10. Wright, 8.

11. Kent Hunter, *Foundations for Church Growth* (New Haven, Mo.: Leader Publishing Co., 1983), 154.

12. Wagner, *Your Church Can Grow*, 113.

13. Barbara Dolan, "Full House at Willow Creek," *Time*, March 6, 1989, 60.

14. Ibid.

4

The Pastor's Role in Church Growth

Most chapters on the pastor's role in church growth begin with a line similar to Peter Wagner's statement, "in America, the primary catalytic factor for church growth in a local church is the pastor." Likewise, Paul Powell says "the most important factor in determining whether a church grows or declines is its leadership; and Lyle Schaller notes, "pastoral leadership is a critical factor in church growth."[1]

Is the pastor *that* important to church growth? And if so, what is it about pastoral leadership which helps churches grow? These are the primary questions addressed in chapter 4.

Little research has been used to back up the notion that pastoral leadership is *the* key determinant of church growth. Some authors use the old standby, "research has shown" to bolster their arguments (without giving any references), while others generalize from the pastor's obvious importance in the largest, most rapidly growing churches in America. Wagner, for instance, challenges readers to evaluate his statement regarding the role of the pastor by taking a look at *Great Churches of Today* and *America's Fastest Growing Churches*.[2] Doing so will show, according to Wagner, that these churches have grown "under the leadership of one person in particular to whom God has given special gifts and who is using these gifts to lead the church to growth."[3]

Church growth seminars, especially those held at large, growing churches, also point to the critical role of the pastor. Well-known pastors describe their own situations and call upon others to emulate the techniques which have worked in their churches. Pastors are told to be strong leaders, to make a commitment to a long tenure, to preach expository sermons, and to focus on evangelism.

Much of what has been said about the role of the pastor in church growth may well be true. But the way to *test* these theories of growth is not to study large, rapidly growing churches as many church growth practitioners have done. Considering only the "superstars" gives a very distorted picture of the type of pastor it takes to achieve rapid growth because these charismatic and talented individuals defy emulation in most cases. In the words of Howard Snyder in *The Problem of Wineskins*, "the church of Jesus Christ cannot run on superstars, and God never intended that it should. There just are not that many, actually or potentially, and there never will be."[4]

Superchurch pastors are unusual individuals, many with great personal charisma and preaching gifts. Much of what they have done is because of *who they are*, and that cannot be copied. So rather than focusing on these churches, research should look at a wide range of growing churches, plateaued churches, and declining churches to discover if there are any characteristics held by growing church pastors which sets them apart from the pastors of churches which are not growing.

In two surveys and in numerous interviews, I have discovered, as did Kent Hunter, that the pastors of rapidly growing churches come in many varieties. Hunter notes,

> A church growth pastor is not just a talented, hard-driving empire builder. On the contrary, various types of pastors head rapidly growing churches. They are not all dynamic preachers. In fact, some preach rather dull sermons! They are not all outgoing personality types. Many are very quiet humble men. They are not all management manipulator wheeler-dealer types. On the contrary, many church growth pastors wouldn't even stand out in a crowd.[5]

The next several sections of this chapter consider various aspects of the pastor's presumed role in church growth. Hard research is brought to bear on each aspect. As will become apparent, conventional wisdom was verified in some cases, while in other cases it is clear that church-growth theory should be revised. The first of these aspects is pastor tenure and turnover.

Pastor Tenure and Turnover

Church growth writers are nearly unanimous in their opinion about long tenure—it helps churches grow. Not only do nearly all large, growing churches apparently have long-tenured pastors, but the suggestion has been made that it generally takes quite a few years to lead a stagnant church to growth. Schaller has said "the most productive years for the typical pastorate are years five, six, seven, and eight."[6] A representative of the Church Loans Division at the Home Mission Board of the Southern Baptist Convention "ups the ante" to ten years: "these churches did not become exceptional until the pastor had served a long term in office—usually ten years or longer."[7] Reeves and Jenson say "it takes a new pastor seven to twelve years to energize an established congregation."[8]

It should be noted that none of these authors appears to be saying that the longer one stays at a church, the more rapidly it will grow. In fact, Schaller also has stated that "there is no reliable evidence to suggest that long pastorates produce church growth." He points to hundreds of plateaued and declining churches which have been served by the same minister for many years as proof.[9]

What these authors seem to be saying is that it generally takes time to get a passive church moving, and if a pastor is able to make it happen at all, it takes at least five years, and maybe far longer.

All of this can be tested, although doing so is difficult and is only really possible in a fairly large denomination with good membership records and ample computing power.

A first step is to look at the simple correlation between length of tenure and church growth. In a survey of growing, plateaued, and declining Southern Baptist churches it was found that *growing* churches were more likely to have pastors with tenure of *four years or more* than were plateaued or declining churches. Conversely, *declining* churches were *much* more likely to have pastors with tenures of *under two years* than were plateaued or growing churches. So it would appear that longer tenure is related to church growth."[10]

The problem with this research finding is that it does not tell us the direction of causation. That is, does longer tenure make growth more likely or do growing churches simply tend to keep their pastors longer? We also do not know whether the rate of growth increases or decreases during a pastor's tenure or whether there comes a time when long tenure becomes counterproductive—leading to a plateau or decline rather than growth.

To examine these issues it was necessary to look at what could be called "pastor cohorts"—groups of pastors who were called during the same year—and follow the growth of their churches over time. In a first test of this procedure, Southern Baptist churches were selected which reported in 1987 that their pastor came to the church in 1977—a tenure of ten years. The growth of these churches was then examined for two year intervals, beginning with their 1975 to 1977 membership change. Results of this analysis indicated that the median percent membership change for these churches was at its lowest level for 1975 to 1977 (the median church declined 1.0 percent, meaning that 50 percent of the churches declined more rapidly and 50 percent did better). Growth then rose substantially to a median gain of 4.2 percent for 1977-1979, and to a median gain of 5.4 percent for 1979-81. Growth then slowed somewhat in 1981-83 to 4.2 percent, before dropping rather drastically to only 2.1 percent for 1983-85 and 1985-87.

The same type of analysis was performed for pastors called in 1978, 1979, 1980, 1981, 1982, and 1983—all of whom remained at the same church through 1987. In each case church growth was lowest in the year the pastor came. Subsequent analysis showed that the year after the pastor came was also generally unproductive. Growth began to pick up in the third year (second full year) and remained high through years four, five, and six, before dropping off in year seven. This suggests that growth does tend to increase along with the tenure of the pastor, but it does not do so indefinitely.

Schaller states that a pastor's most productive years tend to be years five through eight.[11] This research suggests, however, that for *most* Southern Baptists pastors the best years are three through six. The problem, of course, is that the average tenure for Southern Baptist pastors is *less* than three years. Thus, many churches do not experience the best years of a pastorate. Further, the cycle often continues for pastor after pastor and the result is decline. Survey results show that 25 percent of declining churches have had *four or more pastors* in the past decade, as compared to only 5 percent of growing churches.

In the light of these data and from additional information on churches which have grown off the plateau, it would appear that the suggestion of "seven to twelve years to energize an established congregation" is ridiculous as a norm.[12] Research among Southern Baptist churches clearly shows that the majority of churches which *grow off the plateau* began to grow rapidly by the *second year* of a new pastor's tenure. In addition, roughly the same proportion of churches began to grow the *same year* that a new pastor arrived, as churches which took more than five years to see renewed growth.

If revitalization is to occur, it generally occurs rapidly. For some churches the process takes longer, generally six to eight years, but since few pastors stay that long or have the skills necessary to redirect a church satisfied with stability, the proportion of all breakout churches where it took this long is quite small. By contrast, many examples of rapid (but lasting) revitalization exist.

The relationship between pastor tenure and church growth clearly is not as simple as has been suggested in the church-growth literature. The findings can be summed up in this way: rapid pastor turnover hurts growth, and for the majority of pastors, the most productive years for growth seems to be years three through six. However, in those few churches which have been able to grow off the plateau in dramatic fashion, renewed growth generally begins *before* the third year of a new pastorate or after the fifth year.

As most church-growth authors note, most of the largest churches in America do have very long-tenured pastors. It is also true, however, that extremely long tenures (over ten years) are more characteristic of churches on the plateau than of growing churches. So does very long tenure help or hurt? Obviously, *it depends on what a pastor and a church are doing* during the tenure. A new pastor can bring new life, new ideas, and a more objective view of what the church is doing wrong. It frequently takes a few years before the actions of a new pastor make a difference, so an aborted pastorate before the third or fourth year means that a church must wait until two or three years into the tenure of its *next pastor* to realize any growth. On the other hand, pastors who lead a church to rapid, sustained growth are rarely fired. They either stay and build up their present church, or they move to other churches. *So it is no surprise to find long-tenured pastors in churches which have experienced growth.* There simply was no motive for the pastor to leave, either on the part of the church or on the part of the pastor. Thus, very long tenure is more a result of growth than a cause of it.

For most churches *on the plateau*, there is also little reason to change pastors, and even less likelihood of the current pastor being lured away. A plateau is comfortable and normally does not require a great deal of effort to sustain. The members may be happy and nurtured, new building programs are not required, and the pastor may not have to work too hard. Few pastors want to leave such a situation and the result is that plateaued churches are even more likely to have long-tenured pastors than are growing churches.

The Pastor and Evangelism

The fact that a new pastor can often change the entire orientation of a church and lead a plateaued church to rapid growth is evidence of the pastor's importance. The problem is in determining exactly what a pastor can do to help a church grow. In surveys conducted among Southern Baptist churches and among churches in other denominations it has been shown that *few questions* which relate to the activities or characteristics of the pastor are strongly correlated with church growth or decline. Age of the pastor, years of education, seminary training, administrative ability, and time spent in devotional activities were unrelated to church growth, and many other areas of pastoral ministry produced only a marginal correlation with church growth. The clear exception to this rule was evangelism.

The pastors of growing churches tend to see themselves as more evangelistic than do the pastors of plateaued or declining churches, and they tend to do much more evangelistic visitation on average. Growing churches also are more likely to conduct some kind of evangelism training, and the entire ministerial staff is more involved in prospect visitation. This was especially true of churches which have grown off the plateau.

In figure 4.1, for example, it can be seen that the ministerial staff average five or more prospect visits each per week in 61 percent of the growing churches, but in only 30 percent of churches which remained on the plateau does the ministerial staff average this high a level of prospect visitation.

The mobilization of church members to visit prospects and to witness to their friends is even more important to the growth of a church than are the evangelistic efforts of the pastor. But the two should not be considered totally separate. The pastor's involvement in evangelistic activity helps motivate members to participate by reinforcing what has been *said* from the pulpit concerning the importance of evangelism.

In smaller churches which have been languishing on the plateau, the pastor also plays a critical role in *evangelism training* by taking church members on witnessing visits. This is the "pastors plus allies" strategy

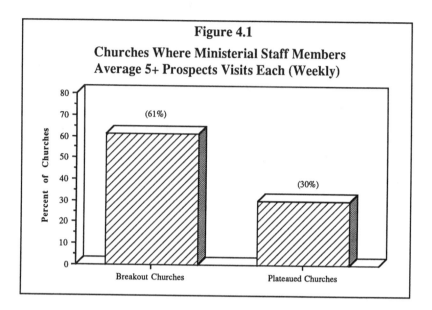

Figure 4.1

Churches Where Ministerial Staff Members Average 5+ Prospects Visits Each (Weekly)

for breakout growth that was mentioned in the first chapter.[13] One of the best ways to break off the plateau is through a reemphasis on evangelism, which is an accepted, though often neglected identity component in most evangelical churches. In smaller churches this reemphasis can be achieved by the pastor recruiting some "allies" who are willing to be trained in evangelistic visitation. This group, plus those whom they reach and bring into the church, can form a core of excited supporters who are willing to visit prospects and work toward revitalizing the congregation.

For larger churches, the pastor's presence in evangelism training is somewhat less important than it is for smaller churches. However, prospect *visitation* by the pastor and staff is *very* important to growth, as is the general evangelistic thrust of the congregation. In other words, the pastor must stress the importance of evangelism; verify its importance by action; and ensure that members are encouraged, trained, and mobilized to visit prospects and witness to their friends. In larger churches, the pastor and a few key allies cannot begin the process of revitalization on their own. The entire church must take on an evangelistic orientation.

Preaching

Pastors tend to put a great deal of emphasis on the role of preaching in church growth. For instance, Paul Powell says, "I am not overstating the case when I say that it is with preaching that churches grow or decline. If you want your church to grow, give attention to preaching."[14] This view is in stark contrast to that expressed by Kent Hunter who says that pastors of rapidly growing churches are not all dynamic preachers. "In fact, some preach rather dull sermons."[15]

Survey data tends to support Hunter more than Powell. Growing churches are more likely to have pastors who are "dynamic preachers," but the relationship is only moderate in strength. It certainly is not strong enough to state that "it is with preaching that churches grow or decline." Good preaching is a positive feature which helps to sustain growth, but it is not something which normally allows a stagnant church to grow off the plateau. No relationship exists between breakout growth and quality of preaching.

Clearly, there are some preachers who may be able to turn around nearly any church through their polished and meaningful oratory. Adrian Rogers, Joel Gregory, and the late C. A. Roberts are a few who have exhibited this gift. Such preachers are so few in number, however, that they do not impact the relationship between preaching and breakout growth. For most churches on the plateau, something far greater than a good Sunday sermon is required for revitalization.

Expository preaching also has been suggested as beneficial to church growth. This seems questionable. Survey results indicate that only a slight difference exists between growing churches and declining churches in this area. The pastors of 52 percent of growing churches say they usually preach expository sermons, as compared to 46 percent of plateaued and declining church pastors. The difference is not statistically significant.

Is there anything about preaching which *is* strongly related to growth? *Apparently the specific content and quality of preaching is less important than its use in imparting a vision, a sense of urgency, and an expectation of spiritual growth.* Expository preaching is not a key to growth, but Bible-centered messages seem to be important. Pastors should foster the expectation that their sermons will help members to understand the Bible and to apply biblical truths to their lives. In order to test this proposition, pastors were asked what percentage of members use their Bibles during a typical sermon. In breakout churches and in the average growing church the percentage of members using their Bibles was much higher than in churches which were plateaued or declining.

Sermons also should be bold, challenging, and enthusiastic. A vision for the future must be articulated and members challenged to play their part in bringing this vision to life. Further, the pastor must be able to create a sense of enthusiasm about the vision, so that members will want to join in its fulfillment.

The average member will forget all of the content and even the subject matter of most sermons within an hour after they were preached. Pastors should keep the message simple—not so members will understand the message, but to ensure that some will *remember it*. The message also should have a point so that there is *something* which can be remembered. Doug Murren suggests that pastors ask themselves "why am I preaching this thing anyway?" along with three subquestions: (1) "what do I want my hearers to know?"; (2) "what do I want my hearers to feel?"; and (3) "what do I want them to do?"[16] If these questions cannot be answered, then a message is unlikely to be heard, much less to have a positive impact on the congregation. Sadly, after many sermons, the worship audience might well identify with this line from an English mystery novel, "that's all one asks of a sermon. No possible relevance to anything but itself."[17]

Pastors should use their sermons to articulate a vision for the church and to reinforce the purpose and priorities of the congregation. New members and uninvolved members who were not directly involved in the creation of the vision, may not understand this dream for the future the first two or three times they hear it, but by the fourth or fifth time it may begin to sink in—that this is what the pastor and members want the church to become. Similarly, if evangelism and Sunday School are part of the church's purpose, these priorities must be stressed over and over so that members will be reminded that the church takes them seriously. And finally, the sermon must be used as a positive motivator. Even when content is forgotten, members will remember the tone of the sermon. Did it make them feel good? Were they inspired? Or were they just bored or browbeaten?

Motivation and Mobilization

A new pastor is normally greeted by a "passive" congregation. Church leaders seem to collectively say "we assume you brought your program with you."[18] Of course, how these same leaders anticipate *dealing* with their new pastor's program may vary widely. A few may be willing to follow the plan to the letter, while in other churches the leaders feel they have "trained" many a young seminary graduate and expect to train many more. They specialize in telling enthusiastic young ministers "it won't work here." In any case, it is the pastor, *not the congregation* who is expected to have the plan.

A church can function fairly well without any particular sense of direction, and in growing suburbs, such congregations may even experience sustained growth. For most churches, however, doing the normal business of ministry, Sunday School, and worship *with no vision for the future* will result in or perpetuate a plateau. The pastor must formulate, or better yet, help the members formulate what various authors have called "a dream," "a vision," or "a great challenge," and then begin to articulate and "sell" this vision to the congregation as a whole. As Powell notes, "we must challenge our people to do great things, otherwise they will stagnate into mediocrity."[19]

Survey results clearly show that the traits of "vision" and "goal directedness" on the part of the pastor are associated with church growth—both in a general church-growth survey and in the survey which compared breakout churches with churches remaining on the plateau. For instance, 40 percent of growing church pastors say that "vision" is one of their traits to a "very great extent" as compared to only 16 percent of plateaued church pastors and 20 percent of declining church pastors.

A compelling vision for the future has the potential for capturing the imagination of the members and providing motivation for action but only if it is "caught" by a large proportion of the congregation. To facilitate this, the pastor must preach and live the vision, and if necessary the pastor must also begin acting on the vision before it has been generally accepted. When things start moving, more and more members may become excited about the possibilities and begin to actively work toward the dream. Throughout this process, continual efforts must be made to develop allies among the existing lay leadership of the church and to create *new leaders* among those who are most excited about the vision. The goal is unity or a "oneness of purpose" around a vision for what members hope the church will become.[20]

The origin of the vision may vary. In some cases it may appear that the pastor has brought in a vision, unilaterally, without the involvement of laity. However, this only seems to work when the pastor is able to tap into an old vision of the church or into a latent sense of purpose. A new vision which does not relate to the identity of the congregation is doomed to fail. In other cases, the pastor leads the laity or enables the laity to formulate the new vision themselves. This is a longer process, but it is necessary in larger churches and also in smaller congregations where the present purpose lacks anything which could be used to revitalize the congregation.

Once a vision has been created, shared, and largely accepted, the pastor must take the lead in moving the church toward new goals which flow out of the vision. Robert Schuller says, "you should be the spark plug. You should be the inspiring commander leading the troops up the hill."[21] No one has ever surveyed pastors about being "spark plugs," but a church growth survey did ask pastors if they were "pacesetters." The pastors in 26 percent of growing churches said that they were pacesetters to a *very* great extent, as compared to only 10 percent of the pastors in plateaued churches and 7 percent of the pastors of declining churches.

The church must allow the dream to impact and enliven all aspects of the church until its identity is transformed. Rather than seeing the church as becoming evangelistic, members eventually will recognize the church as *being* evangelistic. Evangelism becomes part of the role or the "business" of the congregation. Throughout this process of change, and indeed, throughout the existence of the congregation, efforts must be made to keep the dream alive and to keep morale high.

Murren, in a brief article in *Ministries Today*, calls the maintenance of morale, "congregational climate control."[22] It is not viewed as optional. In fact, Murren calls it his "number one role as the pastor in my church." Why? The reason is *motivation* to participate in church activities, to be involved in ministry, and to work toward achieving the goals of the church. People must feel good about what they are involved in, according to Murren.[23] If they do not, all the haranguing and guilt in the world will not keep them doing the necessary activities which cause a church to grow. It bears repeating that a pastor alone cannot do everything necessary to achieve growth. The pastor must provide encouragement, demonstrate enthusiasm for what the congregation has decided that it wants to do, help create opportunities where the desire of members to serve God can be utilized, and help develop a reward system so that the ministry efforts of laity are seen as worthwhile and valued.

In order to examine the pastor's role in building morale, two separate surveys looked at the pastor's ability to "generate enthusiasm." The results were the same. As shown in figure 4.2, the pastors of breakout churches were more likely to say that they "generate enthusiasm" to a great or a very great extent than were the pastors of churches which have remained on stable plateaus. This characteristic is somewhat more widespread in larger churches than it is in smaller churches, but the relationship exists in churches of all sizes.

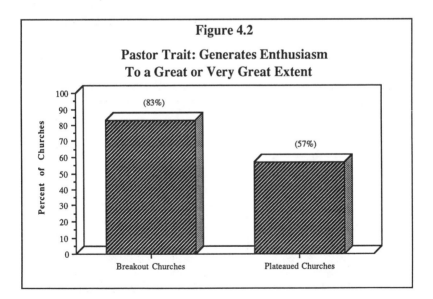

Figure 4.2

**Pastor Trait: Generates Enthusiasm
To a Great or Very Great Extent**

How does a pastor generate enthusiasm and keep morale high? The most obvious and visible medium is the sermon. Positive, challenging, optimistic, uplifting sermons, delivered with enthusiasm are one of the keys—regardless of their objective "quality." *The tone of the message is as important as what is actually said.* Some pastors exude a sense of warmth, acceptance, concern, and optimism. Other pastors are more adept at deflating morale whenever it rears its ugly head. Spiritual "climate control" is not just exercised in the preached message; it also seems to operate through the pastor's efforts to minister to persons in need. The pastors of growing churches tend to be much more involved in *counseling* than are the pastors of plateaued and declining churches. In fact, as seen in figure 4.3, 55 percent of growing church pastors spend at least five hours in counseling sessions, as compared to 34 percent of plateaued churches and 19 percent of declining churches. Growing church pastors do not rate themselves as any more *accessible* than the pastors of plateaued and declining churches (in fact, they are less accessible on average). Still, their greater involvement in counseling seems to indicate that growing church pastors are available when it counts—when members are in need. Further, this relationship implies that the pastors of most growing churches are viewed as concerned about the personal needs of their members and are competent to help.

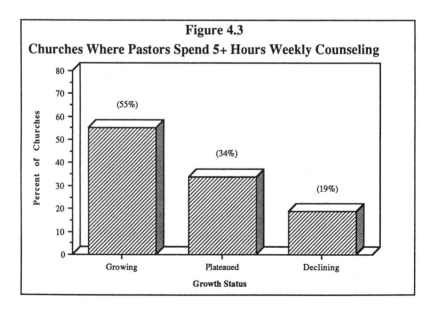

Figure 4.3

Churches Where Pastors Spend 5+ Hours Weekly Counseling

Unfortunately, in some churches no matter how hard a pastor works at unifying a congregation and mobilizing it toward specific goals, nothing happens. Churches have different needs and different personalities; and the perfect pastor for one church may be a disaster in another. As Schaller notes, "[many] congregations are immobilized because the gifts, talents, experience, and skills of the current pastor do not match the needs of that congregation."[24]

It should be noted that if church leaders think that they have a bad match, they should honestly evaluate whether this feeling results from incompatible goals and styles of ministry or from a lack of willingness to cooperate in making necessary changes. In many cases the apparent incompatibility stems from a congregation which is satisfied with their comfortable situation and resists the efforts of a pastor who is trying to mobilize them for ministry and outreach. This is a serious form of incompatibility, but one which calls for a change of attitude on the part of the members, rather than a new pastor who will allow a church to settle for mediocrity. On the other hand, the seeming incompatibility may result from a pastor who is trying to lead a church toward a vision which the members did not create and which they do not understand.

Leadership and Authority

In *Your Church Can Grow*, Wagner has a chapter titled, "Pastor Don't be Afraid of Power!"[25] He assumes, as do many other writers in this area, that in order to lead a church to grow the pastor must have the *power* to do what is necessary.

Wagner goes on to suggest that the pastor's power must be earned, or *legitimized* and thus can be described as "authority" rather than as raw control. It is interesting, however, that Wagner is critical of churches (such as most Southern Baptist congregations) which emphasize a congregational polity. He indicates that the tendency of such churches to oppose strong pastoral leadership on principle will have "to be overcome if the church wants to move to a pattern of growth."[26] Even though a congregational polity allows power to be earned through the demonstration of leadership and competency, Wagner chooses to use churches as his polity models which have been organized around a corporate design, where the pastor is the C.E.O.—"the executive head of the church and the president of the corporation."[27]

The "rule" of Wagner's ideal pastor may "appear as dictatorship or totalitarianism," but he says it is not, because the pastor's decisions are viewed as the decisions of the church members.[28] The pastor of a growing church pastor apparently can be described as a benevolent ruler who only does what is best for his subjects—and they trust him to do so implicitly.

The leader which Wagner describes has been called the "commander" type, and while it is widespread among the pastors of very large churches, it is certainly not universal among these churches, nor is it even the most prevalent form of pastoral leadership among *growing* churches. Still, as Bob Dale notes in his book *Pastoral Leadership*, the commander can be a very efficient style of leadership.[29] Such leaders impose their own goals on the congregation. They are directive, even autocratic. They put goals ahead of persons, production over relationships. It is a model which may "get the job done," but which is widely criticized as theologically spurious.

The commander style is efficient because the pastor calls all the shots and normally has a very limited agenda. The pastor establishes the goals and gives directives to his followers. Demands are clearly defined, as is the authority structure. With a clear vision for the future, the commander-leader can efficiently move a church toward specific goals without costly delays to garner support among lay leaders and without the fear that suggested programs will be rejected.

There essentially are three ways to become a successful commander-type leader. The first is to start a church and structure its constitution to allow this style of leadership from the beginning. The second is to come into a church and *earn the right* to be the commander over a period of several years. The third is to accept a call to a church which has had a commander-type pastor and which expects their new pastor to follow this model. Unfortunately, many young pastors who read books on church growth and who are not afraid of power (they like it) come into churches which have no tradition of commander leadership and *demand* to be given the power to lead the church in the direction in which they believe God would see it go. This is not recommended, because doing so usually results in severe conflict and often leads to the dismissal of the pastor.

It is difficult to test leadership styles using survey instruments, but an effort was made to do so by asking pastors to imagine a situation where members of the church staff or a committee are unable to solve a problem. The pastors were then asked how they would resolve the situation. Would you: (1) act quickly and firmly to solve the problem yourself; (2) work with the group and together try to solve the problem; (3) encourage the group to continue work on the problem and be available for advice; or (4) let the group work out the problem by themselves?

In Southern Baptist churches very few pastors chose the first response, which approximates the commander style (only 3 percent). Those who did so were most likely to be found in growing churches or in *declining* churches. The vast majority of SBC pastors in the survey 90 percent) picked option number 2—a much less autocratic style. Because of this concentration of responses in one category, the relationship between this question and church growth was quite weak. Perhaps because of the congregational polity structure, Southern Baptist pastors are very unlikely to adopt an authoritarian leadership style—and doing so does not appear necessary for growth.

Even though autocratic, commander-style leadership seems unrelated to church growth, it can be said that the pastors of growing churches tend to be *strong* leaders. They lead as quarterbacks—as part of a team—rather than as dictators *or as facilitators*. Survey results in figure 4.4 show that in growing churches 63 percent of the pastors say they view their role as that of a quarterback or ruler (only 3 percent said ruler), as compared to 46 percent of plateaued church pastors and 32 percent of declining church pastors. The majority of nongrowing church pastors say they are either facilitators or "hired hands."

The type of leadership which seems to best characterize the pastors of breakout churches is that of the *catalyst*. According to Dale, the catalyst creates an organizational atmosphere in which positive goals are reached and people are being built up.[30] It is the most effective style because it has a positive impact on the church as an organization *and* on the individual members. Church members are treated as people rather than as functionaries, and yet the work gets done. Goals are established; members feel ownership because they had a hand in the development of the goals; and they are motivated to reach the goals. Catalytic pastors are friendly, vigorous, optimistic, flexible, and persistent. They know what they want to happen, but they understand the axiom, "never use a bullwhip when a smile will do." Things happen in their

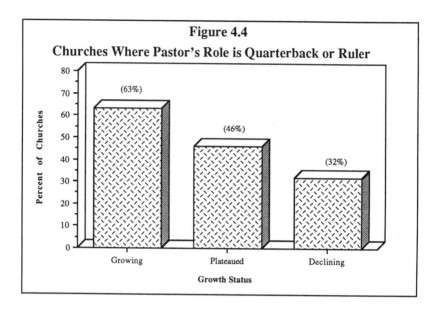

Figure 4.4

Churches Where Pastor's Role is Quarterback or Ruler

churches because they know how to delegate and motivate—and because they have taken the time to educate and encourage those under their leadership.

According to Hunter,

> the church growth pastor sees himself as a player-coach. He participates in ministry, but he sees his primary responsibility as that of training and equipping others so that his ministry is multiplied. In that sense, he is always trying to work himself out of a job. Yet, he never succeeds because his ability to dream dreams always provides him a list of ministries which he wants to pioneer. He trains people because he sees himself as a developer of people.[31]

The catalytic role of the pastor should be clear in all the research findings which have been reviewed in this chapter. Few pastors have the native ability to grow a church primarily through the force of their preaching or administrative acumen. And, in fact, sheer excellence in these areas is not required. Instead, pastors of growing churches are optimistic, evangelistic, and ambitious. They are pacesetters; they place a great emphasis on the Bible in their preaching; and they are able to generate enthusiasm. They direct their churches toward activities which will result in growth.

The impact of the catalytic leader on church growth cannot be denied, even though the sources of the growth can be debated. This is clearly seen when we contrast breakout churches with churches which have continued on the plateau. As will be recalled, breakout churches were on the plateau from 1978 to 1983 and then experienced rapid growth from 1983 to 1987. *The majority of breakout churches in the survey (59 percent) called a new pastor in the same year or in the year before they began to grow off the plateau* (in 1982 or 1983) By contrast, only 21 percent of churches which were on the plateau from 1978 to 1987 called a pastor in 1982 or 1983. Further, by 1987, 43 percent of breakout churches still reported that their present pastor had been called in 1982 or 1983, as compared to only 7 percent of churches which remained on the plateau.

Breakout pastors did not come into a new church, "seize the power," and force their programs upon docile congregations. They inherited churches with problems and were unable to force any issues because they had not earned the right to do so. Instead, they played the role of the catalyst—sharing their vision with the church, linking it to latent purposes which members still shared, creating a sense of excitement, and providing encouragement to those in the church who could see the vision and who were willing to work for it. Results came quickly in most cases and these churches were transformed. No longer did members have to apologize for the sorry state of their church; no longer did they suffer through having to call a new pastor every two years; no longer did they have to attend church because of duty or guilt; and no longer did they wait weeks and weeks before someone was saved or someone joined the church. The church had suddenly become fun and a source of pride; their pastor was not about to leave a church in the midst of its revival; and the testimonies of new members had become a weekly occurrence. This is the catalytic role at its best.

Change, even good change, is threatening to some members, however. But as one layperson said in a once-stagnant, rural church in Arkansas, "It's hard to argue with folks being saved." In other words, changes which result in people coming to Christ are self-legitimating in an evangelical congregation because they tap into a component of its identity. Longtime members may still grumble that the church is not the way it used to be or that they have lost the "say so" in important decisions, but severe conflict is much less likely in an evangelical church when the changes result in growth and an increase in baptisms. This chapter should be good news to the average pastor. No unusual abilities or gifts are required to pastor a growing church. One does not have to be a dynamic orator or a master of administration. On the other hand, one must be committed to reaching the lost and to developing members. A pastor must also have vision. Growing churches are different in character, and that character can be described as "life." Often all a pastor must do to bring a congregation to life is to supply a spark and nurture the flame.

Notes

1. C. Peter Wagner, *Your Church Can Grow*, rev. ed. (Ventura, Calif.: Regal Books, 1984), 61; Paul W. Powell, *The Nuts and Bolts of Church Growth* (Nashville: Broadman Press, 1982), 29; Lyle E. Schaller, *Assimilating New Members* (Nashville: Abingdon Press, 1978), 53.

2. *Decision Magazine* staff, *Great Churches of Today* (Minneapolis: World Wide Publications, 1973); Elmer L. Towns; *America's Fastest Growing Churches* (Nashville: John T. Benson Publishing Co., 1972).

3. Wagner, 61.

4. Howard Snyder, *The Problem of Wineskins* (Downer's Grove, Ill.: Inter-Varsity Press, 1975), 84.

5. Kent Hunter, *Foundations for Church Growth* (New Haven, Mo.: Leader Publishing Co., 1983), 163.

6. Schaller, 53.

7. Robert H. Kilgore, *Projecting Community Response to Determine Church Attendance and Income* (Atlanta: Home Mission Board, 1978).

8. R. Daniel Reeves and Ronald Jenson, *Always Advancing: Modern Strategies for Church Growth* (San Bernardino: Here's Life Publishers, 1984), 24.

9. Lyle E. Schaller, "Pastoral Leadership and Growing Churches . . . Are They Related?" *Church Growth: America* 5 (1979): 9.

10. C. Kirk Hadaway, "Pastor Tenure, Turnover, and Church Growth," *Research Information Report* 2:2 (1988): 1-3.

11. Lyle E. Schaller, *Hey, That's Our Church* (Nashville: Abingdon Press, 1975), 96.

12. Reeves and Jenson, 24.

13. Lyle E. Schaller, *Growing Plans* (Nashville: Abingdon Press, 1983), 22-26.

14. Powell, 51.

15. Hunter, 163.

16. Doug Murren, "Why Am I Preaching This Thing?" *Ministries Today*, November-December 1989, 44.

17. P. D. James, *The Skull Beneath the Skin* (New York: Warner Books, 1987), 287.

18. Lyle E. Schaller, *Assimilating New Members*, 54.

19. Powell, 33.

20. Douglas W. Johnson, *Vitality Means Church Growth* (Nashville: Abingdon Press, 1989), 115.

21. Robert Schuller, "The Key to Church Growth," *Vine Life* 1:2 (1979): 10.

22. Doug Murren, "Congregational Climate Control," *Ministries Today*, July-August 1989, 32.

23. Ibid.

24. Lyle E. Schaller, *Activating the Passive Church* (Nashville: Abingdon Press, 1981), 111.

25. Wagner, 61.

26. Ibid., 68-69.

27. Ibid., 73.

28. Ibid., 68.

29. Bob Dale, *Pastoral Leadership* (Nashville: Abingdon Press, 1986), 42.

30. Ibid., 41.

31. Hunter, 164.

5
The Role of the Laity
in Church Growth

More has been written on the role of the pastor in church growth than on the role of the laity. This is a little odd because it is the nature of the *interaction* between the pastor and laity which ultimately determines whether or not a church will grow. Most church growth experts recognize this fact, but they still tend to place greater emphasis (and write more pages) on the role of the pastor. Lyle Schaller, on the other hand, seems to lean a little more heavily toward the laity because of their ability to *make or break* the plans of the most competent and well-meaning pastor. According to Schaller, "while the pastor is a very important factor in church growth, the critical variable is in the attitudes of the members. [They must] implement those operational decisions necessary to encourage church growth."[1]

In this chapter several topics related to the role of the laity in church growth are discussed. First, it is necessary to look at the *attitudes and orientation* of members, and how they influence the possibilities for growth. Second, the *interface* between the pastor and laity is covered in order to show how this relationship impacts any growth plan. Third, the critical role of *church size* in determining the influence of the laity on church growth is considered. Fourth, *leadership training* and development are discussed. And finally, there is the issue of the *proper use* of lay leaders. As will be seen, the role of the laity in church growth is as complex as it is important.

The Laity: A Thoroughfare or a Roadblock to Growth

In the previous chapter it was mentioned that the pastor was expected to have a plan or a program for the church, and that church members would not develop such a plan on their own. It was also indicated that if the pastor's plan was to have any hope of success it must tap into latent purposes which were part of the congregation's identity. Otherwise, the plan would be regarded as foreign and inappropriate by the laity. Alternatively, the pastor could lead church members to develop a new vision and purpose through a process of strategic planning. If the pastor does neither, however, and the church has no plan nor vision, it will tend to drift along and it will not grow. Such is the case in thousands of churches across America.

It also can be said that the laity will not always *accept* their pastor's dream for the church or even their pastor's role as leader—even though they expect their pastor to *try* to lead the church in some direction. As Peter Wagner notes, "in some churches, not all, a relatively small group of laypeople have gained control of the church and they have decided they will retain it. . . . They intuitively resist allowing a pastor to assume the functional leadership of the church."[2]

Entrenched lay leaders can create such a barrier to change that it seems almost futile to try in many churches. The control of lay leaders can be so binding that in several "breakout churches" growth seemed only possible when a few "key deaths" allowed the pastors to be accepted as leader. Lay leaders who have been members of a congregation for many years view the church as their own. They expect and even demand to have "say so" in every major (or even minor) decision. Newcomers, *including the pastor and staff* are suspect because they have not earned the right to call the church "mine" and also because they do not understand what it is about the church which old-timers hold dear. So the issue is not just control, it is the fear that the church will become something different and foreign—something that they will not like.

The threat posed by a new pastor and also by an influx of new members is something felt most acutely in smaller congregations. Survey results show, for instance, that in smaller congregations older members were more likely to feel threatened by newcomers than was the case in larger congregations; and it was also found that this feeling of threat was more of a detriment to church growth among smaller congregations than in larger churches.

The family atmosphere is very important to the laity in smaller churches. Growth in the form of newcomers (rather than through children of members) threatens this atmosphere in two ways. First, it brings in a large number new people whom the current members *do not know*. A few each year would not be a problem, but more than that disrupts existing networks and creates strains in communication. Newcomers must be absorbed into social groups within the church, and they also must learn the informal rules of interaction and behavior. Second, it is feared that growth will eventually make the church so big that the family atmosphere will be destroyed—that the church will reach a point where everyone cannot know everyone else.

Growth is disruptive and uncomfortable for lay members who want their church to be as comfortable as possible. In fact, the need for a nurturing, caring congregation may overshadow and constrain the motivation for ministry and outreach. As Schaller notes, "significant numerical growth in the congregation that has been declining or on a plateau for years inevitably means change. The faster the growth, the greater and more disruptive the changes."[3] This is felt so deeply that in many growing congregations the members have seen enough of growth—they do not want any more. In a survey of Presbyterian laity, for instance, in response to the question, "is increasing members good?" the members of growing churches were more likely to say "not at all" or "a little" than were members of stable or declining churches. By contrast, members of declining churches knew they needed growth in order to ensure future vitality and tended to say that increasing members was good.[4]

The key factor in determining the role of the laity, and especially of lay *leaders*, as a help or as a hindrance to church growth is *attitude*, not competency. Douglas Johnson notes, "the first characteristic sought in lay leaders in vital churches is that they have a basic positive attitude. They are willing to listen and to change."[5] This was clearly demonstrated in survey findings. The laity in growing churches are future oriented rather than past oriented. They are influenced but not bound by tradition. They are open to innovation; they are willing to change; and they are willing to follow the leadership of their pastor.

As shown in figure 5.1, the pastors of 54 percent of growing churches said their members lean towards "dreaming about the future" rather than "living in the past," as compared to only 21 percent of plateaued churches and 15 percent of declining churches. In growing churches, and in churches which have the potential to grow, the laity are not satisfied with the status quo. They want to reach others with the gospel, and they know their church can do a better job at doing so. In other words, change is welcome if it is consistent with their perception of the purpose and goals of the congregation.

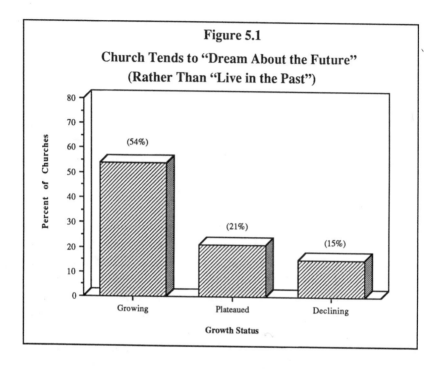

Figure 5.1

Church Tends to "Dream About the Future"
(Rather Than "Live in the Past")

Pastors should not assume that their congregation is basically apathetic and that it is up to them to instill a positive attitude and willingness to "pay the price" on the part of their members. As Paul Powell says, "don't underestimate your people. Most preachers would be surprised at the response of their people if they would just lay before them a great vision or challenge."[6] In many cases the desire is there, latent among the laity, waiting for a pastor to awaken it by suggesting what the congregation might become, to build it up by encouraging and empowering the laity, and to channel it into action by giving the laity responsibility for the future of their church. Too many pastors assume that because the desire is not evident in actions, it does not exist.

Members do not want change for the sake of change, of course. They will only feel that change is warranted if it will further the work of the kingdom of God. But some churches do not want change for any reason, and it is the attitude toward change which is especially critical among churches on the plateau. Survey results show, for instance, that in 57 percent of breakout churches the "willingness to change" has become "more characteristic," as compared to only 25 percent of churches which remain on the plateau. When a willingness to change is present in a church and the members share a sense of optimism about the future, the battle for growth is half won. All a church may require for breakout growth is a pastor with the skills, vision, and drive to lead the church toward new growth-producing goals.

When members do not want change and when they resist giving the pastor the authority to lead, then great care must be taken to involve large numbers of laity and to build consensus among older members before a church acts. A good example of this can be seen in the decision of a church in rural South Carolina to tear down an unused and dilapidated, but very historic, old sanctuary. Keeping up the structure was a financial drain on the church, and its very presence seemed to keep the congregation looking toward the past. The pastor thought the building had to go, but rather than trying to force the issue and confront the objections of older members, he led the church to create a task force to consider what to do about the structure. And rather than creating a representative group which would likely pit older, long-term members against newer, more progressive members, he led the church to create a task force composed primarily of older members. When the direction of the church rested in their hands they were compelled to consider the situation objectively and with the greater good of the congregation in mind. They decided to recommend that the old structure be removed. This decision can be viewed as a turning point, after which the church became oriented toward the future, and soon it began to grow.

The Pastor-Lay Interface

The pastor's primary function in leading the laity to build a growing church is by providing motivation, inspiration, and encouragement, and by leading the church to consider its mission and then to develop or reinforce a compelling vision for the future. With a vision providing the goals, and with ministries in place to accomplish the goals, the pastor assumes the role of a quarterback who calls the plays (a player-coach, but not just a coach). The pastor is always involved but does not "carry the ball" on every play. This role also requires the continued use of "climate control" techniques to motivate members who, while committed to the goals of the church, may grow weary of their particular roles in the pursuit of the goal (the church equivalent of an offensive line).

The relationship between the pastor and the laity is one of reciprocity. The pastor must be able to motivate and inspire the laity, but *the laity must also be willing to let their pastor lead.* Peter Wagner says it well, "If a strong pastoral leadership role is as important as I think it is, a strong followership role for the people is equally important. . . . I have talked to many a frustrated pastor who wants to lead the church to growth but cannot because the people in the church refuse to grant permission."[7] This takes trust, a good match between the pastor and the laity, and the willingness of powerful lay members to let the pastor lead. *This does not mean giving the pastor blind obedience, however.* The pastor may be a shepherd, but this does not mean that laity are sheep. We are all called by God to be ministers, and this implies responsibility. Further, pastors are capable of mistakes and a system should be in place to ensure that new ideas (whether from the pastor or from the lay leaders) are carefully examined before they produce irreversible actions with negative consequences. At the same time, the laity should not stand in the way of new ideas and actions which are designed to reach people with the gospel. If they do not trust their pastor's leadership, then they have either called the wrong pastor (and should get one they can trust), or they are a congregation which simply refuses to be led by anyone.

Survey results indicate a moderate relationship between breakout growth and the pastor's perception of the "willingness of church members to follow pastoral leadership." The correlation might have been stronger if it were not for the "halo effect" which seems to operate when questions are asked about the pastor's relationship with the laity or when laity are asked to evaluate their pastor. A majority of pastors *say* that members are very willing to follow their leadership and a full *90 percent* of pastors say they have a good working relationship with lay leaders (in both growing and nongrowing churches).

Another component of the lay-pastor relationship involves the issue of delegation (and acceptance) of responsibility. The pastor, especially in larger churches, must be willing and able to delegate responsibility to the laity. Conversely, the laity must *allow* the pastor to delegate to them and accept responsibility for ministry, outreach, and the assimilation of new members.

Wagner notes, "some pastors feel that laypeople aren't qualified for ministry because they have had no professional training in seminary or Bible school. Some are threatened by the possibility that a layperson could minister in some area better than they could."[8] In some small, docile churches it is *possible,* though not wise, for the pastor to assume nearly all responsibility for leadership, ministry, and outreach. In larger churches, doing so is clearly impossible, but many pastors take on too much and refuse to relinquish *responsibility* for ministry, even though they are compelled to delegate the *tasks* of ministry. According to Johnson, "some pastors . . . feel that they have the training to make the church work and that laypersons are there only to support and follow them. Fortunately, this attitude is not present in vital congregations."[9] The effective pastor who is interested in building up people, as well as in building up the church roll, will delegate authority, responsibility, and as well as tasks. And if the church does not currently have many in leadership who are willing to accept such responsibility, the effective pastor will find willing members who have the desire and the proper positive attitude, if not the skills, to do the necessary jobs.

In many churches, and especially in small congregations, the laity have the view that ministry is "what we pay the pastor for"—that it's not our responsibility. When the pastor of such a church issues a challenge to the lay leadership the response is likely to be silence, or at best a half-hearted affirmation such as, "we must help our pastor to do his work."[10] The pastor is seen as the hired hand who was employed to do all the "God stuff." The people in the church carry on their traditional roles, and the pastor does everything else. This is a comfortable pattern for stability and decline in the small congregation, but not for growth— either numerically or spiritually.

A further problem is that the pastor is expected to be a "pastor" to all members in a small congregation. The church which sees itself as a family expects family-type concern from their pastor. When someone is sick, they expect to be visited by the pastor, not by another staff member or their Sunday School teacher. They also expect the pastor simply to drop by now and then to see how they are getting along. Doing so is possible in a small church, but as a church begins to grow it becomes less and less feasible. The pastor must move from the role as shepherd to that of a rancher. This is a difficult, wrenching process, which may alienate some members of the congregation who liked the church better the way it was. Pastors of small growing churches should be ready for a backlash from long-term members, and spend more time pastoring these individuals and in trying to get them involved in the process of change.

The Critical Role of Church Size

Church size plays an important role in determining how the pastor, the laity, and the interaction between the two, impacts church growth and church revitalization. In smaller churches the pastor has certain constraints and opportunities which do not exist in larger congregations. Similarly, in large churches there are advantages and disadvantages which relate to church growth that small congregations do not have. The pastors of large and small churches are dealing with *entirely different organisms*, and as such, different strategies are required to keep churches growing and to move stagnant churches off the plateau.

In smaller churches the keys to growth are to be found in the pastor and in the ability of the laity to withhold power. Wagner says about small churches, "a pastor can do all the preaching, the teaching, the administration, the counseling, the committee meetings, the fund raising, the mission program, the community relations, the visitation, and the outreach activities almost singlehandedly."[11] Small size makes this possible, and it allows the pastor as the central focus of ministry in the church to stress (or not stress) the things which can cause a church to grow. All that is needed, according to Schaller is "the active support of only a handful of members and the passive permission of the rest of the people."[12]

If lay leaders withhold permission in a small church, the pastor can do nothing, but if they grant even tacit approval then it is possible for the pastor to tap into dormant purposes of the church, gain a few allies and begin the process of revitalization. Nowhere is this more evident than when a new minister comes to a small church which is willing to change. According to Schaller, "the likeliest candidate to initiate this strategy [for change] is the just-arrived 'new minister,' who possesses the freedom of the outsider, still has some discretionary time every month, holds the authority that goes with the office of pastor, has no stake in maintaining the status quo, possesses a strong evangelistic concern, and has gifts and skills in the process of planned change."[13] If a pastor is able to capitalize on newness, to "unfreeze" the situation, and to institute the necessary changes, growth is likely to occur. By the time the pastor's eighteen-month "honeymoon" is over, a "new church" has been created which cannot easily revert to what it once was. In addition to a new spirit and vitality, new leaders will have emerged and at least some of the older leaders may have shifted from tacit approvers to wholehearted supports of the new or renewed vision for the future.

In small churches which have been through this process of rapid change, some backlash is likely to occur. This may take the form of older members dropping out or of an actual power struggle over control of the future of the church. The greater the change, the greater the likelihood of a backlash. In interviews with some breakout church pastors it was found, however, that the pastor is not always aware that anyone in the church resents the changes. All they have heard is that their members did not like being on the plateau and were very glad for the changes which had occurred.

In small churches a strong core of spiritually mature lay leaders is not necessary for renewed growth, nor is the presence of evangelistic zeal. The keys are permission on the part of the laity and the proper plan and ability to motivate on the part of the pastor. Because of this, among smaller congregations, variables related to the *pastor* tend to produce strong correlations with growth, while variables which deal with the character of the *laity* produce very weak correlations with growth.

In larger churches the situation is entirely different. Although new pastors are a key to breakout growth in larger churches (just as they are in smaller churches), the pastor cannot change the direction of the church with the help of just a few allies. Strong, supportive lay leaders are required, as is a great willingness to change. Tacit approval is not enough in the large church. Lay leaders must help create the plan and work for its success, or it will not happen.

The important role of the laity in the breakout growth of larger congregations is clearly seen in figures 5.2 and 5.3.

In figure 5.2 it can be observed that the relationship between breakout growth and a rating of lay leadership is stronger among larger churches than it is among smaller churches. The difference on this question between larger breakout churches and larger churches which have continued on the plateau is *47 percentage points,* as compared to a difference of only 13 percentage points among smaller congregations. Large churches which have been able to break off the plateau are characterized by very strong lay leadership. Large size requires the delegation of authority and responsibility, and in growing churches the pastors apparently are able to delegate, and lay leaders are able and motivated to accept responsibility.

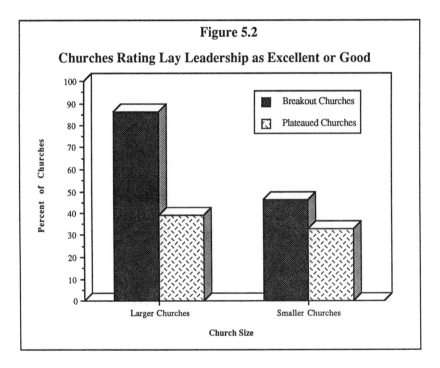

Figure 5.2

Churches Rating Lay Leadership as Excellent or Good

Not only must a large church have relatively strong lay leaders in order to see growth occur—the laity as a whole must be *willing to change.* They cannot be so bound by tradition that they are unable to imagine being something different from what they presently are. There can be no new dream if this is the attitude of the laity. As can be seen in figure 5.3, among larger churches a full 91 percent of breakout church pastors say that "willingness to change" has become more characteristic of their congregation in the past several years, as compared to only 31 percent of the pastors of larger continued plateau churches— a difference of *60 percentage points.* A moderate relationship between this variable and breakout growth also can be seen among smaller churches, but its magnitude is not nearly as great as was observed among larger congregations.

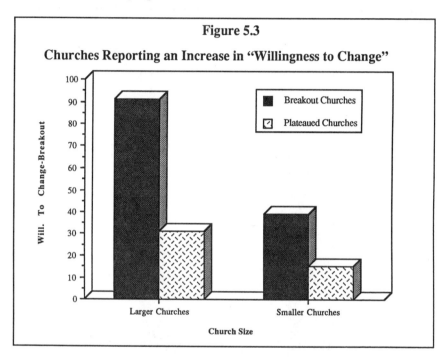

Figure 5.3

Churches Reporting an Increase in "Willingness to Change"

The actions necessary to lead a large, stable church to growth will depend greatly on the character of the laity. Many churches have all the institutional mechanisms and lay leadership necessary to achieve growth, but they are leaderless or are embroiled in conflict of some type. Such churches have "pent-up" growth, and only need for a pastor to supply some leadership, direction, and healing in order for the church to "take off." Many of the larger breakout churches were of this type. They had been well-staffed for years and had put into place all of the organizational components recommended by denominational program leaders. Lay leaders had been trained, committees were in place, and the institution was sound. But the church wasn't moving. Some congregations are satisfied with this sort of stability, but others are not.

They want to do something, but they do not know what or how. Into such situations, a new pastor, or a renewed pastor is able to galvanize the church into action behind a vision for the future, which may already exist among the laity in latent form.

When large churches do break off the plateau they are usually of the type described above, with "pent-up" growth waiting for the proper motivation and leadership. In many larger churches, however, pent-up growth does not exist, nor is the congregation ready to be led. Because of this, breakout growth rarely occurs. As indicated earlier, survey data clearly show that if churches are going to break off the plateau, they tend to do so very quickly (within the first two years of a pastorate) or else it takes much longer (after at least five years). There are almost no examples where breakout growth began during years three through five of a pastor's tenure. The explanation for this finding is in the need for change.

Where pent-up growth is not present, the pastor of the large church must begin the slow process of education and change. This cannot happen quickly. According to Schaller, "in the large church, the pastor or the senior minister usually has to take a very active aggressive role in building the capability to reach, attract, and assimilate new members into each organization, board, class, circle, committee, and group in that large complex organization."[14] The need for evangelism and outreach must be awakened. Mechanisms for new member assimilation must be created or revived. Individual members and the groups of which they are a part must learn how to be friendly and accepting of newcomers. Lay leaders, accustomed to a role as power brokers, must learn how to minister. When these and other changes are in place, then, and only then, can a pastor begin to lead the church to growth. Making changes takes time and usually requires that a church confronts its reason for being.

Leadership Training and Development

"The first responsibility of the pastor is to prepare people to minister for Christ," according to Powell.[15] Even if the pastor can "do it all" in some church settings, this is not the pastor's proper role. The laity must be trained to be ministers, and opportunities for ministry must be created by them and for them. The emphasis in too many churches is on teaching, rather than on training. The difference should be clear. Members are trained in order to *do something.* This does not mean that members become programmed automatons. Training is an interactive process whereby members gain knowledge and skills, and then create their own unique ways of applying what they have learned in ministry.

All churches have leaders, but they may not have the kind of leaders which are needed for church growth. Many persons who take on leadership roles are not interested in ministry. Instead, they seem only concerned with the maintenance of the organization. Why cold, mean-spirited persons are motivated to serve in church leadership roles is hard to understand, but they are there in force, ready to greet you with a blank look or an insincere smile.

Pastors who are interested in growth must look beyond sour-faced members who appear to live a theology of works, beyond the perpetual naysayers, and beyond the entrenched traditionalists to "persons who are positive, conscientious, and more spiritually motivated."[16] Motivation and attitude apparently are more important than skill. Skills can be acquired, but a positive attitude is a deeply ingrained trait, and spiritual motivation is less often taught than caught. A pastor is much better off training those who already have positive attitudes than in trying to change the attitudes of those who already have some skills.

Many persons who have both a desire to minister and the motivation to do so have seen their ideas and hopes for change squashed by negative church leaders. They are unlikely to be found among the existing leadership of a stagnant church, and it is up to the pastor to seek these persons out and recruit them for leadership roles. If they are convinced that they can make a difference, then they are likely to respond to such an invitation.

The next step is to create an *atmosphere* in the church were service is seen as valued and significant. Through the articulation of a vision for the future and with the purpose of the church continually reinforced by the pastor, staff, worship leaders, Sunday School teachers, and others, the laity will begin to see themselves as part of a vital enterprise which is moving toward definite goals and having an impact on people's lives. As described by Johnson, "laypeople in these churches, besides having a positive attitude about themselves and their church, want to be leaders in the church for the sake of witness and service. They prepare for leadership, and they take their positions seriously. They give time to learn."[17] This new atmosphere also will impact the attitudes of the nay-sayers. They may come to realize that their negative opinions are no longer valued, and that there may be something positive about the course the church is taking.

Without a stable (and growing) core of positive lay leaders, it will be impossible for a growing church *to keep growing.* New programs and ministries can be staffed by existing dependable leaders for a time, but the potential for burnout is ever present. Such individuals may not say "no" to an important task, but when a major job ends they may actually leave the church for another. Churches should have a process in place which identifies, recruits, and trains potential new leaders so that existing leaders will not become overburdened.

Ethnic churches often take leadership training more seriously than do anglo churches. Many have on-going leadership training classes which are *required* if someone desires to teach Sunday School or lead a organization of some type. At First Chinese Baptist Church of Los Angeles, the process of training may take several years before someone is allowed to be the senior teacher in a Sunday School class. Expectations and requirements are high for teachers, and yet the church apparently has no difficulty in attracting persons to its university-style classes for potential leaders.

The development of new leaders is also part of the genius behind the growth of Paul Cho's home cell group ministry at Yoido Full Gospel Church in Seoul, Korea. In each home cell group, a new leader is always being trained. When the existing group grows too large and must divide, the trainee then takes over leadership of one of the "daughter" cell groups. Then the process repeats itself. This type of cellular division is only possible through a routine process of leadership training. It ensures a continual supply of new leaders, some of whom may stay in their role as cell group leader, while others may be given additional responsibilities to oversee a number of home cell groups.[18]

The Proper Use of Lay Leaders

A final point regarding the use of lay leaders concerns the tasks which they are called to perform. As Charles Chaney and Ron Lewis stress, "care must be taken to avoid giving maintenance responsibilities to (lay leaders) who have interests in growth through outreach."[19]

Unfortunately, there is a tendency to use the best leaders, whatever their gifts or interests, in jobs which the secular world would view as high status—primarily involving finance and administration. These jobs need doing, but a church should not use its best teachers and evangelistic visitors in tasks which essentially involve the maintenance of the organization.

There are many worthy goals and activities for a church to pursue. In fact, the possibilities are so great that many churches can easily neglect those activities which result in professions of faith and membership growth. Maintenance activities must be done, but this should not mean that Sunday School outreach, evangelism, and dynamic worship only receive the support which is "left over." On the contrary, growth and ministry related activities must be built into the structure of a church and receive attention before maintenance activities—not after. The purpose of the church is not to maintain itself, or to keep itself from dying. Its purpose is ministry and missions; and the laity, like the pastor, should place more stress on supporting these activities than on keeping the machine "oiled and running." Further, roles should not become so differentiated that those who have gifts and interests in maintenance, ministry, or outreach should come to see other responsibilities as outside their role. All members must work to assist in the everyday functioning of the church. Similarly, the responsibility for ministry and evangelism is incumbent for all church members, whether they are part of a formal team in these areas or not.

Notes

1. Lyle E. Schaller, "Foreword" in *Church Growth Strategies That Work*, Donald McGavran and George G. Hunter III (Nashville: Abingdon Press, 1980), 8.

2. C. Peter Wagner, *Leading Your Church to Growth* (Ventura, Calif.: Regal, 1984), 67, 69.

3. Lyle E. Schaller, *Growing Plans*, rev. ed. (Nashville: Abingdon Press, 1983), 45.

4. General Assembly Missions Council, *Membership Trends in the United Presbyterian Church in the USA* (New York: United Presbyterian Church, USA, 1976).

5. Douglas Johnson, *Vitality Means Church Growth* (Nashville: Abingdon Press, 1989), 46.

6. Paul W. Powell, *The Nuts and Bolts of Church Growth* (Nashville: Broadman Press, 1982), 32.

7. Wagner, 63.

8. Ibid., 57.

9. Johnson, 48.

10. Powell, 78.

11. Wagner, 55.

12. Schaller, *Growing Plans,* 63.

13. Ibid., 23.

14. Ibid., 63.

15. Powell, 79.

16. Johnson, 47.

17. Ibid., 49.

18. Paul Yonggi Cho with Harold Hostetler, *Successful Home Cell Groups* (Plainfield, N.J.: Logos International, 1981).

19. Charles Chaney and Ron Lewis, *Design for Church Growth* (Nashville: Broadman Press, 1977), 51.

6
Setting Goals and Making Plans

The typical church in almost any American denomination is either on a plateau or declining in membership and participation. Rapid growth is atypical, and among older congregations the pattern is even more pronounced—plateau and decline are the rule; growth is the rare exception. This should come as no surprise to church leaders at the associational or local judicatory level. Looking at the churches in their own associations, conferences, or synods, they are well aware that membership plateau has become the norm.

Unfortunately, some church leaders do not view the large proportion of plateaued churches as a particular problem. In a recent state conference, one official reacted negatively to the way the term "church on the plateau" had been used in recent years. He said that he preferred to employ the term "stable" because it was a more "positive" label. Plateaued churches were not actually declining, he argued, so they should be seen as reflecting health and stability within the denomination—not as problems to be addressed by denominational agencies.

From a purely statistical perspective, this official is probably right. Plateaued churches are stable. The large majority remain on the plateau for years, growing a bit one year, declining some the next, but basically "holding their own." From a perspective of mission and vitality, however, most plateaued churches have serious problems. They do not *expect to grow*. They do not *plan to grow*. They are directionless.

This does not mean that the church on the plateau is failing to do good things. Most are. They may be very warm and friendly congregations. They may also have ministries in place which benefit members and which impact the local community in positive ways. Further, the pastor and laity in these churches may be working just as hard as their counterparts in growing congregations. Yet there is something lacking.

The organization is not going anywhere, it is only seeking to maintain itself, rather than striving to become something *better* and to reach even *more* persons with the gospel. Goals, when they exist at all, tend to be maintenance oriented rather than dealing with membership, attendance, and outreach. This displacement of mission goals with maintenance goals results in fewer conversions and baptisms, less community ministry, and less excitement than is normally found in growing churches. In the worst situations, members may use the term "dead" or "lifeless" to describe their church.

There is value in holding onto what is good in a church—in maintenance. The identity of a congregation must be translated into institutional forms which provide vehicles for ministry and outreach. Still, a congregation should never be satisfied with what it is. An identity and a vision should lead to goals, which should lead to further goals that build on what has already been accomplished. A church which seeks only to be what it presently is will stagnate and become what it never intended.

A Natural Tendency

In his book, *Parish Planning*, Lyle Schaller makes two useful generalizations concerning the "natural tendency" of organizations to become directionless. First, he says, "every organization tends to move in the direction of redefining purpose in terms of institutional maintenance and survival. . . . The care and feeding of the organization, rather than service to the clientele, tends to become the number one priority in the decision making process." Second, "any organization, but especially the voluntary nonprofit organization, that does not have tangible, highly visible, definable, and measurable goals tends to turn toward institutional maintenance as the primary concern of the organization."[1]

As Schaller notes, the problem is worse in voluntary nonprofit organizations, but it should be added that it is worse still in voluntary nonprofit organizations with *diffuse rather than specific purposes and goals.* Although the church can be seen as a "life saving society" (as in the often-used illustration of the sea rescue society which becomes a social club), its goals are much more diffuse than those of the International Red Cross, Mothers Against Drunk Driving, or other voluntary nonprofit organizations which were organized for very specific purposes. A church can still be a *church* even when it ignores some of the major reasons for its initial formation. It may even come to the place where it operates more as a religious social club than as a New Testament church—but this does not mean that people stop seeing the institution as a church.

The process through which an organization loses its sense of purpose is often described as a phase in the organizational "life cycle." The fact is, however, that organizations, unlike the human body, are not required to proceed through a cycle of growth, declining energy, and eventual death. Organizations can continue as lively, growing organisms for hundreds of years, as long as there is a market for their product, a sensitivity within the organization to the needs of their clientele, and a willingness to change in reaction to market conditions.

There may be a *natural tendency* toward goal displacement and the preoccupation with institutional maintenance, but this tendency can be resisted in any organization. *Effective organizations* are in a constant process of self-evaluation, asking themselves "what are we doing right, what are we doing wrong, and what new priorities need to be added in the light of our stated purposes and the changing conditions under which we operate?"

Churches normally begin life with clear purposes and goals. Typical among Baptist congregations is the purpose of reaching new community residents and assimilating them within a strong Sunday School. Additional goals are added along the way, such as a new educational wing or a larger sanctuary, but most churches eventually reach the point where the major goals have all been reached. The church has achieved stability and has held the long-awaited note-burning ceremony. The Sunday School is strong; although as the community has aged, it is likely now to be dominated by adults rather than children. With its major purpose achieved, such a congregation tends to settle into a maintenance mode. It drifts along without any clear sense of direction and can continue to do so indefinitely.

For rural churches the pull toward a goalless existence is stronger than any other setting. Everyone in the area is aware that the church exists, and with a stable or declining population in most cases, there is no great impetus for aggressive outreach to new residents. Further, frequent pastor turnover, entrenched lay leadership, and the long-established traditions which are so typical of rural congregations mean that a reevaluation of purpose and the development of new goals are unlikely to occur.

Since churches are so resilient, and because they are meeting the needs of their most committed and supportive members, it is very possible for a church to remain "passive" for decades without any danger of dying. Many large, urban churches are of this type, as are most rural and small-town churches and many congregations in older urban and suburban neighborhoods. They may be known for their cooperative nature and for their support for denominational programs, but they are not likely to be known for reaching the lost or for growth.

A Redefinition of Purpose

One of the main reasons that churches do not set membership and attendance goals is that they have seen the process fail miserably. In a church which I once attended, the pastor decided to have a competition between our church and church of similar size and prominence in another city. The contest was for the highest cumulative Sunday School attendance over four Sundays. The loser had to send their choir to sing at the winning church. Even though the contest was promoted by the pastor and within each Sunday School department, I got the impression that no one cared whether we beat the other church or not. My church lost and attendance during the month rose no higher than would have been expected during that time of the year.

I had a similar experience as a member of a long-range planning committee. After over a year of work, the plan was presented to the church and adopted with relatively little discussion. Three years later, few of the goals were pursued, much less accomplished.

The problem in both cases was a directionless church attempting to goad itself into action by formulating goals—before it had redefined its purpose or role. In the first situation the goal was seen as the pastor's, not that of the church. In the second situation the goals were seen as those of the long-range planning committee, again, not of the church. Schaller notes, "a new role must be defined before meaningful goals can be formulated and implemented. Attempts to formulate and implement specific operational goals in the absence of an agreed upon and widely supported definition of a new role usually produce frustration, and/or division, and/or apathy."[2]

In other words, goals must be consistent with and flow out of the accepted purpose of a church. If a church does not see itself as an aggressive, evangelistic church which desires to grow, it will be futile to set membership and attendance goals. Apathy will be the typical reaction among most laity—leading to frustration on the part of the pastor and any laity who are committed to achieving the goal. In fact, pastors may be tempted to leave an apathetic church after trying and failing for several years to prod the members into action by setting goals and holding special events.

Peter Wagner has commented, "churches that really want to grow will set bold goals for growth."[3] This may be true, but someone reading this statement would be misled by thinking that the most important truth deals with goal setting. It does not. There are three points here and they are of equal importance. First, a church must want to grow. This speaks of purpose and identity. Second, a church must set goals which translate that purpose into action. Disembodied goals don't work. Third, in each step there must be ownership and involvement on the part of the laity. A purpose which only belongs to the pastor will result in goals that only belong to the pastor. Members will work toward goals which they own.

Growing churches have a desire for growth and they act in a purposeful manner to achieve growth. As can be seen in figure 6.1, survey results show that 69 percent of growing Baptist churches score high in the desire to grow among their members, as compared to 32 percent of plateaued churches and 42 percent of declining churches. Similarly, in figure 6.2 it can be seen that 57 percent of growing churches tend to be "purposeful" rather than "drifting," as compared to 19 percent of plateaued churches and 27 percent of declining churches.

Growing churches are not aimless; they have a sense of vision and purpose. It would be possible for this purpose to neglect growth, of course, but in the case of growing churches, the purpose includes the desire for growth. Interestingly, it is the church on the plateau which is most aimless and is least likely to desire growth—not the declining church. Perhaps this should not be surprising. The easiest course for a church is no course, and a membership plateau makes this possible. The church gains a few members here and there; it has a few baptisms;

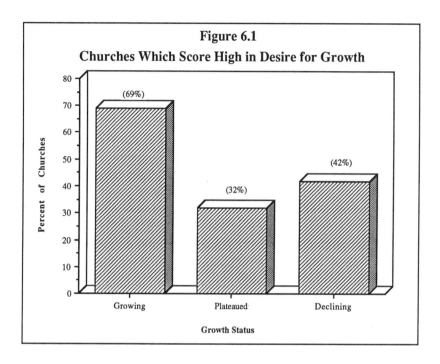

Figure 6.1

Churches Which Score High in Desire for Growth

and it can maintain an impression that everything is fine. The declining congregation, on the other hand, has no such illusions. Members understand that things cannot continue in this manner indefinitely, lest the church die. So for this reason, it is likely that some declining churches have made the first step in redefining their role—they now have a desire to grow and a sense of what they want to become. They want to turn their decline around and a new purpose is the necessary first step.

The Pastor's Role in Identity Transformation

The pastor plays an important part in the redevelopment of a congregation's identity. In fact, without the active involvement of the pastor it is unlikely, if not impossible, for a congregation to develop a new compelling role for itself. The manner in which the new role or purpose is developed and the part played by the pastor may vary greatly, however, according to the style and gifts of the pastor, the size of the church, and the orientation of the members toward change.

In many churches the pastor may initiate the process of redefinition, and may appear to "unilaterally define the new role."[4] A new pastor or a "renewed" pastor develops a "vision" for the future and begins to preach it, teach it, and sell it to the congregation. The pastor may even begin to act on the vision before it is generally "caught" by a large proportion of the laity. As noted earlier, however, this approach only works if the new role is able to tap into latent elements of the congregation's identity. In other words, it may be possible for a pastor to help a church which is doing little evangelism to redefine itself as an evangelistic congregation, but only if evangelism is valued by most of the congregation. For a pastor to attempt a similar "unilateral redefinition of role" in a congregation which did not place any value on aggressive evangelism would be ministerial suicide.

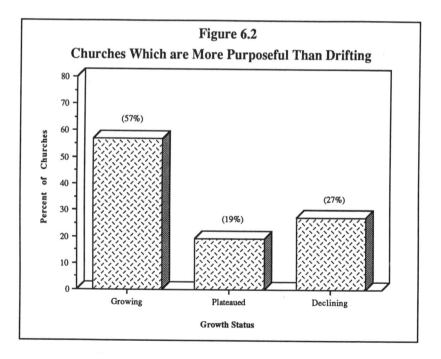

Figure 6.2
Churches Which are More Purposeful Than Drifting

In one congregation which I visited last year, the pastor arrived with the intention of building an evangelistic church. The congregation was a typical, aimless, small-town First Church, but it eventually became a church on a mission, actively reaching its community for Christ. From the day he arrived, the pastor preached about the need to visit, to witness, and to share the good news of Christ with anyone in the town or surrounding countryside who would listen. He also began to visit prospects, neighbors, lapsed members, and newcomers to the area. A number of long-term members joined with him in this activity. People were saved, baptized, and welcomed into the fellowship of the church. New Christians also joined with the pastor and his allies in visitation and evangelism. More were saved and the church began to grow rapidly.

Even though a number of long-term members did not like some of the changes which were occurring and did not immediately accept the pastor's vision for the church, they held back their criticism because evangelism was seen as having value in this congregation. And even though the church did not have a clearly defined role as an evangelistic church, evangelism was a latent element of the congregation's identity—which provided legitimacy for the efforts of the pastor to redefine the role of the congregation. The church eventually came to see itself (its redefined role) as an evangelistic congregation by *acting* like an evangelistic congregation. The pastor played the critical role in this process, and now his job is to lead the congregation to establish and reach challenging goals which flow out of their new sense of purpose.

For many other churches a much different process toward a new definition of role or purpose would be required. The pastor's part is that of a facilitator and of an organizer, rather than of the source of the redefinition. For instance, a pastor might create the opportunity for a new vision by exposing church leaders to a dynamic church which is anything but directionless. A long-range planning committee could visit: (1) churches in their area which had broken off the plateau; (2) churches known for their exciting worship; (3) churches with effective evangelism programs; or (4) rapidly growing congregations. This may create a sense of excitement among lay leaders about what their church might become. The excitement can then be channeled into a process in which a new vision for the congregation is created by the pastor and the laity.

In other situations, a crisis of membership decline, racial/ethnic/age transition in the community, urban renewal, airport expansion, sudden population growth in exurban areas, and so forth, might prompt the call for action. In such situations, the pastor and lay leaders might ask for intervention on the part of a church consultant or a denominational agency to help them deal with the process of change. An intervention strategy would help the church determine its options for the future. These options could then form the basis for a redefinition of purpose.

Finally, the pastor could play a major role in calling for and assisting a long-range planning committee or the church council in working through a redefinition of purpose. This may be a lengthy process where the laity and pastor struggle with where the church is and where they would like to see it go. The process also may involve an intervention. In a growing United Church of Christ congregation in Massachusetts, for instance, the planning committee had been meeting for six months before bringing in a consultant from Hartford Seminary. She has agreed to advise the planning committee for a period of eighteen months, as they develop a new vision, share the vision *as it is developing* with the rest of the congregation, and eventually construct specific plans for becoming the kind of a church they wish to be.

The Role of Strategic Planning

All churches do some planning, if only to schedule special services, fellowships, revivals, a pledge commitment day, and so forth. But this is not what is meant by strategic planning. Strategic planning involves the evaluation of ministries and priorities of a church with the intention of either redirecting its orientation or refining its existing programs.

For most aimless, passive churches the need is not for refinement, it is for redirection. Such congregations need a renewed sense of purpose, a new definition of role, and intentionality with regard to their priorities. But this is not always apparent to church leaders—especially those who have been reared in passive churches. They may think treading water is the normal state of affairs, rather than intentional action and planned change. Evaluation of the current direction of the church and its existing priorities may be required to make members aware of the need for change.

Evaluation can proceed in many ways and use a variety of resources.

One of the best ways to determine the current priorities of a church is to look at how it expends energy and money. As Kent Hunter states, "the way the church spends its *energy* is another good test of its philosophy of ministry." Such an evaluation may well reveal that a church has "far too much activity without purpose, majoring in minors and overlooking priorities."[5] In other words, a church may be focusing primarily on activities related to institutional maintenance and ignoring its stated priorities (assuming that it has stated priorities).

The first step for a planning committee or a planning task force is to evaluate the overall direction of the church. What has been the role or purpose of the congregation? Has this purpose been made superfluous by the maturation of the congregation, the achievement of early goals, or by a changing context? Is the church failing to act on its priorities? Even more basic questions may be asked. What is the purpose of any church? The answers to these questions will determine whether or not a church should begin the process of redefining its role or if it only needs to reestablish its stated priorities as *real* priorities which shape and direct the work of the church.

Bill Sullivan suggests that long preparation for growth may be counterproductive because all of the energy and enthusiasm can be dissipated in the process of planning. When the time finally comes to act on the plan, the inspiration and drive have evaporated. He counsels churches to "do it now."[6] I would argue that this is true when a new minister is attempting a "pastor and allies" approach to growth off the plateau or when a church is simply reaffirming a well-accepted purpose. In these situations it is not wise to waste too much time before beginning action on short-term goals. On the other hand, church leaders would be foolish to try to "do it now" before an accepted new definition of purpose or role had been developed—especially in medium-sized and larger congregations. A more appropriate strategy would be to build continual feedback between planning task groups and the larger congregation into the long-range planning process so that excitement builds rather than dissipates over time.

After evaluation comes the definition of purpose—either in new form or as a reaffirmation of an existing purpose. This purpose should be developed by the pastor and by a planning committee with a large amount of input from the larger congregation. It should be a product of the whole congregation. Connected to the statement of purpose should be priorities or broad objectives which form what is best called a "vision" for the future of the congregation. This vision must then be allowed to infuse all aspects of the congregation until it becomes central to the identity of the congregation. Program strategies and goals then can be developed out of the priorities and move the church from planning to action.

Does a planning process which involves evaluation and a long-range plan correlate with church growth? The answer is yes. Survey results show that 85 percent of churches which have grown off the plateau have reevaluated their programs and priorities during the past five years, as compared to 59 percent of churches which have remained on the plateau. Similarly, 40 percent of "breakout churches" have developed a long-range plan, as compared to only 18 percent of continued plateau churches.

The relationships between planning activities and breakout growth are fairly substantial, but they are not quite as strong as those between goal setting and church growth. This was not surprising, because as noted earlier, many churches plan but they do not do strategic planning. Further, simply having a plan on paper does not mean that it is owned or being followed, nor does it mean that any growth-producing strategies and goals have been developed. For planning to impact growth, the process must establish growth as a priority, include goals which orient church action toward growth-producing programs, and motivate people to work toward achieving the goals.

The Role of Goal Setting

"Some churches do not plan at all. Whatever happens just happens and no definite course of action is followed."[7] This is not the case for most growing churches, however, and certainly not for churches which have been able to suddenly grow after years of stagnation or decline. Growing churches are goal-directed. They set measurable goals for attendance, Sunday School classes, membership, revivals, and for many other areas.

Survey results shown in figure 6.3 indicate that 69 percent of growing churches set membership goals, as compared to only 42 percent of plateaued churches and 32 percent of declining churches. Goals also are part of the process through which passive churches become active. One of the strongest correlates of "breakout growth" was a question dealing with whether or not goal setting had received increased or decreased emphasis over the past several years. As can be seen in figure 6.4, 64 percent of the breakout churches report such an increased emphasis on goal setting, as compared to only 26 percent of churches which remain on the plateau.

Setting goals helps churches to grow. The next obvious question is why? And there are a number of answers. Goals provide direction and ensure that priorities (which flow out of purpose) are acted upon. When priorities include growth, goals ensure that growth-producing actions occur. *Challenging* goals have the *potential* for producing motivation and enthusiasm. Big plans create a sense of excitement if they are consistent with the mission and vision of a congregation and are not seen as totally impossible. Goals add "handles" to the purpose and priorities of a congregation. They provide a concrete way for members to see themselves making the vision become a reality. Goals also open doors for people to express commitment and they encourage the emergence

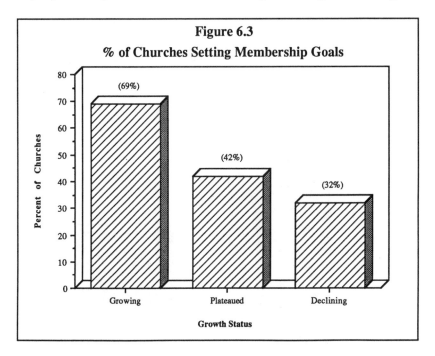

Figure 6.3
% of Churches Setting Membership Goals

of new leaders. Goals strengthen the identity of a congregation by providing tangible proof that the church is becoming the "thing" which was visualized in its statement of purpose. Finally, goals reinforce the future orientation of a church. They turn attention away from triumphs of the distant past and away from a fixation with maintenance. Goals have the *potential* for all these things, but they are not automatic.

Goals often fall flat. No one becomes motivated, no one works any harder, new people do not become involved, and if the goal is not reached, no one cares. Why does this happen? The most frequent reason is that the pastor or a planning committee tried use the goal as a way of motivating a passive congregation rather than as a vehicle for the expression of its new vision. "Disembodied goals" of this sort can provide motivation, but only if they are "sold" with great enthusiasm by the pastor, and *only in smaller churches which accept this style of*

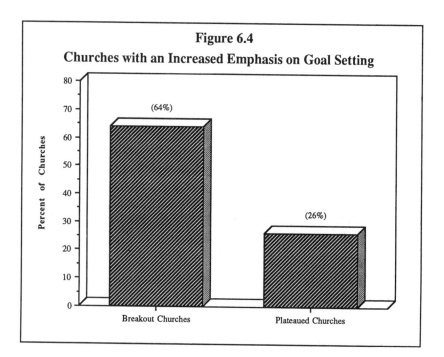

Figure 6.4

Churches with an Increased Emphasis on Goal Setting

pastoral leadership. In larger churches there is simply too much institutional resistance for a disembodied goal to overcome. The pastor can try to whip up enthusiasm, but unless lay leaders had a hand in the development of the rationale and unless they see the need for the goal, they will not "pass it on," nor will they process it through the various mechanisms which make or break a goal in a large church. In a denominational agency the situation is even worse. Goals may not reach the individuals who are critical to their success, and are thus unable to generate the necessary action.

Goals are often set too low. If there is the feeling that "we will meet this goal without trying," then it will not inspire or motivate anyone to do anything or give anything out of the ordinary. Mission-giving goals which are set through reference to increases in the consumer price index are good examples of goals that challenge no one.

Goals also can be set too high. A goal can seem so absurd that no one will work to achieve it. For example, at a Campus Crusade for Christ planning retreat some years ago, an estimate was made as to how many persons each individual at the retreat would have to contact per day in order to share the gospel with everyone in Memphis within one year. A goal was set to do just that, but it was too overwhelming. No one even tried to accomplish the goal.

Goals must be set properly in order to have any chance of being reached. This means that goals should be related to the shared purposes, identity, and priorities of a congregation. In addition, the goals should be challenging, important (rather than trivial), and measurable. Great effort should be made to promote the goals and to ensure that everyone hears about the challenge—several times, and in several different settings. If the congregation had a definite part in the definition of the church's purpose, this process of "selling" will not be hard. Members will immediately understand why the goals are important. Finally, operational procedures must be put in place so that the necessary tasks will be accomplished to support the goal, and so committed members will know how to become personally involved in the effort.

A congregation can have many goals, but if it wishes to grow, at least some of its goals must deal with growth-related issues. This is not to say that all of the goals in a church should deal with membership, enrollment, and attendance. They should not, because even though growing churches do tend to set goals in these areas, their priorities also include reaching people for Christ, producing spiritually mature Christians, and meeting human needs. Growing churches are effective churches, and their goals tend to be well-rounded rather than having a single-minded focus on growth.

Through planning, evaluation, and goal setting it is possible for a church to avoid or at least smooth out the typically cyclical nature of growth in most congregations. Rather than the normal road from purpose to aimlessness to a wrenching reformulation of purpose, churches can "schedule, in advance, periodic review and evaluation."[8] They will know when priorities are being pushed aside by maintenance activities, when goals are in danger of not being met, when new programs need to be added (or old ones eliminated), and when the vision of the church is dimming or is unrealistic in light of where the church and its community are heading. In other words, a process of periodic review and evaluation helps a church stay on track, moving toward its vision, and also to recognize when its direction must be altered.

For small churches the tendency is to set no goals, and for larger churches the tendency is to set meaningless goals which motivate no one. The challenge for stagnant churches, large and small, is to reestablish purpose and direction, to set the church in motion, and to see that the direction continues.

Notes

1. Lyle E. Schaller, *Parish Planning* (Nashville: Abingdon Press, 1971), 95.

2. Lyle E. Schaller, *Activating the Passive Church* (Nashville: Abingdon Press, 1981), 80.

3. C. Peter Wagner, *Your Church Can Grow,* rev. ed. (Ventura, Calif.: Regal Books, 1984), 56.

4. Schaller, *Activating the Passive Church,* 82.

5. Waldo Werning, *Vision and Strategy for Church Growth* (Chicago: Moody Press, 1977), 56.

6. Bill M. Sullivan, *Ten Steps to Breaking the 200 Barrier* (Kansas City, Mo.: Beacon Hill Press of Kansas City, 1988), 45.

7. Charles Chaney and Ron Lewis, *Design for Church Growth* (Nashville: Broadman Press, 1977), 34.

8. Schaller, *Parish Planning,* 103.

7
Attracting Visitors
(And Making Them Feel Welcome)

In a society where church membership is not assigned or required, the problem of how to attract visitors becomes critical. People comparison shop for churches in America and half the battle is getting potential "customers" through the door of your church on Sunday. A church must be able to attract a steady stream of visitors because only a small percentage of those who visit will eventually join; and because this is a very mobile society, a regular supply of additions is necessary in order for churches just to stay even and avoid decline—much less to start growing.

It also is essential for churches to make a good impression on those who make it through the front door. All congregations think they are friendly and welcoming, but some are deluding themselves. How do visitors feel about your church? Are they impressed by the warmth and friendliness, by the number of greetings, or do they think to themselves, "Well, they weren't particularly friendly there, but the service wasn't bad, and the church *is* convenient." Most churches don't know how they impress visitors, or they only know how they have impressed those who have joined. But what about those who have not joined? What did they think about your church? Such questions are not trivial. How they are answered may be essential to the long-term health of your congregation—so they should be asked.

Sources of Visitors

Almost every book on church growth which mentions the major sources of new members quotes research concerning the percentage of new members who joined or first visited because of an invitation from a friend or family member. The results appear so consistent that it is safe to say that a majority of people attend a church for the first time due to this sort of invitation.

There has been a tendency to confuse the issue of visiting and joining churches, however. People *join* churches for a wide variety of reasons, and in most cases they are barely able to articulate the key reason why they joined. In personal interviews, new members will supply a *list* of factors which together formed a "critical mass" that precipitated the decision to join. Surveys which force new members to pick "the most important reason why you joined" will produce data, but rarely is there a single reason for joining a church. Visiting, on the other hand, is a simple matter. In interviews or in surveys, persons are able to say why they visited for the first time. Responses will include "a visit from the pastor," "a friend at work invited me," "my neighbor invited me," "I picked it out of the phone book," "I saw it while driving by and decided to give it a try," and so forth. Reasons for visiting a church are not complex, but reasons for joining can be *very* complex.

If the major reason that people visit a church is the invitation from a friend or family member, and if invitations from friends take on even greater significance in growing churches, what does this say to churches as they seek to increase the number of visitors who attend their worship services? Does it mean that churches should constantly remind their members to invite friends, coworkers, and neighbors to church? Yes. Does it mean that churches should hold special events where each member is encouraged to bring at least one friend? Yes. But it also should be noted that the ability of a church to attract visitors through word of mouth has much less to do with admonition, encouragement, and programs to encourage invitations to friends, than it does with the quality of worship, the appealing character of the congregation, and with the fact that members in vital churches care about persons who are outside the walls of their building. Together, these factors make the invitations come naturally. So rather than spending much time asking what can we do to get our members to invite their friends to church, we instead should determine whether or not there is anything about this church which is so good that people will want to tell others about it and whether or not a true sense of caring for others exists within this congregation.

Some churches have a preacher who is "the best in town." Other churches have worship services which regularly provoke a sense that "we have encountered God." Still other churches are so warm and accepting that even newcomers feel like they have found a "family" who cares about them as people, rather than as projects or numbers. There are many other special qualities which a church can exhibit, and if the quality is sufficient, members will tell others about it. You can't keep them quiet.

Sadly, many churches do not have anything which members can identify as a specialty, or if they can, the specialty is not good enough to encourage members to say to their friends, "You should see this! You just won't believe it—I'll pick you up." If your church lacks the quality which encourages natural invitations, the first step should be to ask "why" and then the congregation should begin the process of upgrading its specialties or *developing* a new specialty, rather than worrying about how to *compel* members to tell others about their church.

If members do not care enough about others either to talk with them about Christ or to invite them to visit their church, then the problem is even more serious. A congregation in this sad state must take a new look at what it means to be a church and what it means to be Christian. Only when the congregation becomes a church again and only when members recommit themselves to being Christians can the congregation begin to reach out to others with hands that seek to give and hearts that offer acceptance and love.

Other Ways to Get the Word Out

It would be foolish for a church to rely *solely* on word of mouth in order to attract visitors. Even though this route is more efficient in terms of response, a church should not neglect other ways of attracting visitors, even though a much smaller proportion of those contacted, invited, or who hear about the church will ever attend. Churches must reach beyond the limits of their own networks to the larger community of dropouts, to people whom I call *Mental Members* (persons who identify with a church or denomination, but who rarely, if ever, attend), and to that small group of Americans who were reared with no church identity.[1] Together these groups make up the unchurched population, which should be the major outreach focus for any evangelical church.

Many vehicles have been suggested for churches to get the word out to unchurched persons, to newcomers in the community, and to people who are searching for a new church. Some are not always successful, but most can be helpful if done in the right way.

One of these vehicles is *publicity* through newspaper ads, direct mail to nearby residents or prospects, radio and television spots, billboards, news releases about special events and other church activities, and so forth. Lyle Schaller has indicated that church leaders should tell their finance committee, "experts on church growth suggest that a congregation that is serious about numerical growth should allocate at least five percent of the total expenditures for newspaper advertising, direct mail . . . and other forms of advertising."[2] Five percent may be the appropriate percentage for a church to spend on publicity, but research into this issue suggests that almost no church comes close to that level of spending. Further, the percentage spent on publicity is only weakly correlated with church growth. Survey results show that 51 percent of growing Southern Baptist churches spend 1.1 percent or more of total receipts on publicity, as compared to the 40 percent of plateaued churches and 38 percent of declining churches who spend a similar amount. Raising the cut-off level from 1.1 percent to 2 percent or to 3 percent of total receipts for publicity does not increase the difference between growing, plateaued, and declining churches. There simply is a weak relationship.

The problem is that any church with money can do publicity, and the motive behind these efforts is not always pure, nor is the quality or method of publicity always appropriate. For many churches the motive is to attract new members so they will support the church financially or help turn around a decline in membership. Publicity efforts to attract visitors to a church which has no vitality may succeed in terms of drawing visitors, but the publicity will not result in growth, because only a very small percentage of the visitors will wish to join a "dead" church.

Churches can spend large amounts of money on publicity which may actually repel rather than attract visitors. For instance, I recently saw a rather bizarre television ad for a church which featured a pastor standing next to his fishing boat. He said, "I'm standing at the shore of this lake about to go fishing. As I stand here I realize that these fish are a lot like us—not always obedient. And the only way we can become obedient is through Jesus Christ." The pastor then identified his church and invited everyone to visit. It is hard to say whom such an ad might attract. My fisherman friends thought the spot was not well done because they consider fish to be uncooperative, not disobedient, and I suspect most unchurched people in that city (perhaps like the fish) prefer disobedience to this pastor's idea of obedience.

All churches should have a regular newspaper ad and most should pay the nominal fee for a larger than normal ad in the yellow pages. The proportion of visitors who seek out a church primarily because it is close by and of their denomination is relatively small, but this avenue should not be ignored. Advertising at this level should be considered a minimum in terms of publicity.

Churches also should be aware that free advertising is available in the form of public service announcements on radio and television. Churches can use these announcements to promote community ministries or special events which may be of interest to local community residents. This avenue may allow a church to attract more unchurched persons to its facilities for a seminar than it ever could through a traditional revival.

Churches should consider developing four-color brochures about themselves and mailing them to community residents. This activity produces a stronger relationship with church growth than does the percentage of total receipts spent on publicity. As seen in figure 7.1, 53 percent of growing churches have sent out a brochure or other mass mailing to community residents, as compared to only 28 percent of plateaued churches and 33 percent of declining churches. This action also appears to be more important to the growth of larger churches than it does to smaller congregations.

Other actions which are designed to attract first-time visitors include church bazaars or festivals, a religious census, and welcome visits to new community residents. An out-of-the-way United Methodist church near Nashville, Tennessee, holds an annual catfish fry/craft fair/fundraising auction each summer. Attendance at the festival grows every year and for the past several years has totaled several times their average attendance on Sunday morning. The event lets community residents (and potential visitors) know the church is there, that it has friendly members, and that they would be welcome if they decided to attend.

A religious census appears to be a particularly useful strategy for attracting visitors and developing prospects for churches which are trying to break off the plateau. Often such churches have not done any

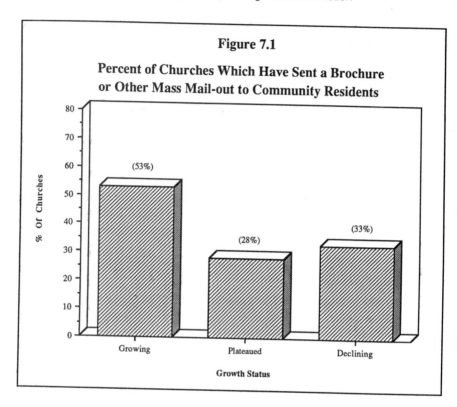

Figure 7.1

Percent of Churches Which Have Sent a Brochure or Other Mass Mail-out to Community Residents

outreach for years. They are known in the community as "dead churches," and if they even have a prospect file, it is in hopeless shape. A community census lets residents know that the church is interested in them, and it allows the church to develop an up-to-date prospect file with viable prospects. By working such a file through mailouts and additional visits, many people may be persuaded to visit the church.

Ministry activities also can be used as vehicles for drawing people into relationships with church members, and these relationships may result in additions to the church family. By reaching out to meet needs through literacy classes, conversational English classes, support groups of various kinds, and mission action, a church shows the community that it cares. This may attract persons who are in need of these services as well as persons in the community who want to join with the church in its ministry efforts.

Finally, most growing and plateaued churches visit new residents to the community. Declining churches do not, however. Like newspaper ads, a yellow pages listing, and public service announcements, this activity should be automatic for most churches. Research has shown that new residents are more likely to convert, drop out, or switch denominations than are persons who live in a community all their lives.[3] It is up to the churches in the community to see that a move creates the opportunity for greater commitment to the church rather than an opportunity for less.

What Is Irrelevant?

Buildings do not attract many visitors. The fact that most evangelical denominations lack a Crystal Cathedral or soaring Gothic architecture may have something to do with this, but even in the most beautiful churches, there is a big difference between visitors who come to look and visitors who come to shop. Churches need more shoppers and fewer lookers.

Unfortunately, there is a tendency for plateaued and declining congregations to put the blame for their membership problems on things other than themselves. An old, unattractive sanctuary can be a convenient object of blame, which often leads to a building program or a move to the suburbs. Rather than constructing an attractive sanctuary which will suit their current attendance and allow for modest growth, such churches tend to overbuild. Since members feel that their current facilities are the obvious source of their problems, it is assumed that once this deficiency is overcome, the church will begin to grow rapidly. Thus it would appear foolish to build a facility which will only seat their peak attendance. Instead they build a sanctuary which is double or even triple their *average* worship attendance.

Few churches will *admit* to what Schaller calls "architectural evangelism"—expecting one's beautiful facility to draw and captivate visitors.[4] But it should be stressed that any tendency to put hope in the ability of a building to attract people is dangerous. Typically, a church will end up with a defeated congregation rattling around in a sanctuary which is less than one third full and saddled with a large debt. This, in turn, may lead to cut backs in growth-related programs. There is no reason why church facilities should not be attractive and well constructed, but space should be viewed as space which will only be filled through the actions of church members, not through its mere existence.

It follows that the visibility of a church, the quality of grounds, and even the condition of the sanctuary are virtually unrelated to church growth. A church is slightly better off if it is visible, if it has attractive, well-landscaped grounds, and if it keeps its sanctuary painted and spruced up. Other things are far more important, however. Out-of-the-way churches can overcome their poor locations through the efforts of the pastor and laity to let others know about their church; whereas highly visible churches may neglect efforts to contact new residents or to encourage members to invite their friends. "Everyone knows the church is here." Yes, everyone may know, but if they do not receive a personal invitation, they are unlikely to visit.

Finally, a team of greeters seems to be more of a "good thing" a church can do to try to make people feel welcome than it is a key to church growth. A person in this role may be viewed by visitors as a functionary who is being friendly under duress, rather than because he or she is *really* happy to see the visitor. With this in mind, churches should choose naturally friendly, outgoing people for the greeter role who will look for visitors and guide them to a Sunday School class, to a greeting station, or to the proper door of the sanctuary. Many churches use anyone who will agree to the task, even persons who look past you to the next person as they are shaking your hand. At one church I attended the "official greeter" never recognized me nor would he say "hello" in any other setting, even though he shook my hand every week for seven years. Visitors are attracted to a friendly church. Greeters can add to this sense of friendliness, but in most cases they are a nonfactor.

Making Visitors Feel Welcome

It is not enough to attract visitors to your church. They must be made welcome if a church hopes to convince them to join. In rather crass terms, the shoppers who have been drawn to the store must be convinced to buy. And in the case of a church, they must be so convinced of this outlet's product that they want to buy into the company.

Initial impressions are important to the visitor, and they are often neglected by most congregations. This is due to familiarity, rather than lack of concern, however. Long-term members know where everything is, where to park, the proper doors to the sanctuary, and so forth, and they assume that everyone else does also. For this reason, I would estimate that well over half of the churches in America lack signs which identify Sunday School classes, which give directions to an information center, or which direct visitors to the sanctuary. It is a game churches play called "find the right door." Visitors already feel confused and a little ill at ease in a new church, and we seem to do our best to aggravate these feelings.

Try to imagine the reactions of first time visitors. You might even make a game of it with an out-of-town friend. When you drive up, is the proper entrance to the parking lot easily identified, and is it clear where to park? For larger churches, and especially for larger, growing churches, parking is a real problem. And even though crowded lots will tell a visitor that "something good must be happening here," some visitors will become frustrated if they arrive a little late and cannot find a place to park. Growing churches tend to have special parking for visitors, and it is a good idea to have a sign near the entrance of the parking lot indicating that reserved spaces are available.

When visitors get out of their cars what do they see? In most churches they see several closed doors with no signs and no one to direct them to a Sunday School class or to the sanctuary. If visitors are lucky they may be able to follow members who seem to know where they are going and ask directions: or visitors can hope that there will be someone inside who is assigned the task of assisting visitors. Greeters help in this situation if they recognize that their most important responsibility is to identify potential visitors and direct them to where they need to go, rather than simply to act friendly and open doors. Why churches neglect this aspect of dealing with visitors is a mystery. Signs are cheap and organizing an effective team of greeters in parking lots or near the various entrances to a church is easily accomplished.

Once a visitor has entered the church and has been directed to a Sunday School class or a visitor's center, what happens next in your church? Often, the visitor's center is staffed by cold, businesslike people who took the job because filling out forms makes them feel like they are helping. The emphasis here should be on the welcome, not on processing a file. Friendly, outgoing people who know almost everyone in the church should be at these stations. They should give the visitors the warmest greeting they have ever received, personally take the visitors to a Sunday School class, and introduce them to another very friendly person. Does this happen in your church, or do you require visitors to sit alone until someone notices that they look unfamiliar?

It is important to make sure that visitors can park, that they are not confused about where to go for Sunday School or worship, that they receive several genuine welcomes upon arriving at the church, and that they are not ignored in a new Sunday School class or department. The most critical factor, however, is somewhat less tangible: *the sense of warmth and friendliness which visitors feel from a congregation.* As Douglas Johnson notes, "one difference between a vital and a not-so-vital congregation can be measured by how many people welcome new-comers and regular attenders. . . . It is a warm and friendly greeting, not superficial."[5]

Congregations can be placed on a continuum from cold to warm with respect to how they treat visitors. Most churches fall somewhere near the middle of this continuum, but a few churches lie on either extreme. On the side of this continuum which is to be avoided are those "exceptional" congregations which actually are cold and a little rude to new-comers. When visitors are late, ushers may say "you know we start at 10:45" and act a little put out about having to find them a seat. If the visitors are early they may find themselves occupying the traditional seat of a long-time member and might be asked to move. Sunday School leaders will spend a great deal of time getting visitors to fill out cards and then neglect to introduce them to members. The bulk of churches are not this rude to visitors, however. Members just ignore visitors or make superficial attempts to make them feel welcome. Greeters will have no idea that the people are visitors and make no effort to direct them to the right place. Instead, they will shake the visitor's hand and move onto the next person coming to the door. In Sunday School classes a few persons will shake hands and say "hello," but no one will try to engage the visitor in a meaningful conversation. In worship the visitor will be recognized and handed yet another card to fill out. No effort is made to have members greet visitors who are sitting near them, and after the service no one thanks them for attending.

The situation is entirely different in a minority of churches which seem unusually warm and welcoming to newcomers. In the Sunday School newcomers are immediately taken up by members who intro-duce them to others and who engage them in conversation which seem to express an interest that goes beyond the usual superficial pleasantries. After Sunday School members will invite visitors to sit with them in worship, and may even extend an invitation for Sunday lunch. In worship, people notice visitors and welcome them. Often, churches will ask all of the members to stand up, and then everyone welcomes each other—with visitors receiving many more expressions of welcome than anyone else. There is also a sense of warmth within the worship service itself, which as Johnson notes, "seemed natural to attenders, but it takes a great deal of work and pastoral care to create such an attitude in the church."[6] The service is consciously designed to demonstrate that "we care" and "we accept you." This attitude is seen in the music, the announcements, in the greeting to visitors by the pastor, in the sermon, and in the actions of members attending.

Survey results underscore the relationship between expressions of love for visitors and church growth. As seen in figure 7.2, 88 percent of growing churches were rated by their pastors as being very loving to visitors as compared to 59 percent of plateaued churches and 62 percent of declining churches. This shows that even though few churches think of themselves as unfriendly to visitors, a loving attitude is nearly universal among growing congregations.

How do visitors feel when they attend your worship services for the first time? Is your church one of the many which have decades-long practice in the skill of discouraging outsiders from uniting with the church, or is it one of the even larger number of congregations which "has all the bases covered" with greeters, a welcome center, and the like, but is only superficially friendly?[7] To find the answers to these questions, don't ask yourself—ask new members and recent visitors. Did the new members join the church in spite of the welcome they received, or, at least in part, because of the welcome? And did the welcome extended to visitors seem typical or were they impressed by its sincerity and warmth?

Follow Up

Visitors are always impressed when the pastor or another representative of a church calls on them at home within a day or two after a visit to the church. Churches which have weekly Monday night visitation have a real advantage in this area, because people are almost shocked

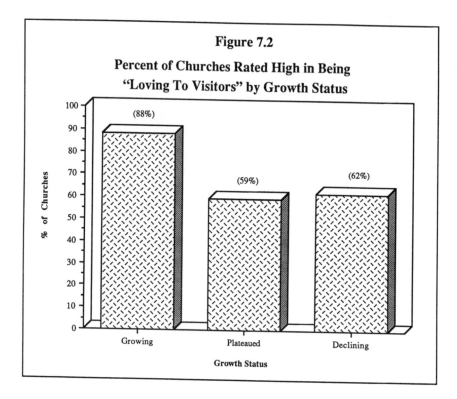

Figure 7.2

Percent of Churches Rated High in Being "Loving To Visitors" by Growth Status

to receive a visit the next day from members of the church they attended on Sunday. In fact, in interviews with active church members in several churches which have Monday night visitation, many mentioned how impressed they were to receive a visit so quickly. In the visitors' minds it showed that the church was both organized and interested in them. It was a definite point in the favor of these churches and many new members were added because this one feature set them apart from other churches in the area.

It also is true that active church members who move to a new city and visit a church are often amazed when all they receive is a brief letter, or at most a phone call during the following month. Regardless of how friendly the church seemed, the lack of a follow-up visit is taken as evidence that the church really is not interested in them.

Unfortunately, many churches have very poor follow up. The names of those attending on Sunday are added to an unwieldy and not up-to-date prospect file. During the next month someone will thumb through the cards for the monthly visitation effort, but if not enough members show up for visitation the visitor may not receive a contact for well over a month—if ever. The prospect file continues to grow and the likelihood of rapid follow up of visitors grows less and less.

A visit in the home (or an invitation to lunch or some other personal contact) with someone who visits your worship service should be made within one week. Schaller recommends visiting within forty eight hours.[8] It also appears to be important to make *multiple* visits to newcomers. A quick visit shows that the church is organized and that it cares. Several more visits or personal contacts (lunch, dinner, a coffee break, etc.) show that the interest of the church is more than superficial. The newcomer can only think, *they really want me there*. It is then up to the newcomer to respond with further visits to the church or with rejection of the church. For churches which actively make the effort to visit those who have recently attended their Sunday School or worship services for the first time, the response is usually to return.

Notes

1. See C. Kirk Hadaway, *What Can We Do About Church Dropouts?* (Nashville: Abingdon Press, 1990), chapter 2.

2. Lyle E. Schaller, *Growing Plans* (Nashville: Abingdon Press, 1983), 106.

3. C. Kirk Hadaway and Wade Clark Roof, "Those Who Stay Religious 'Nones' and Those Who Don't: A Research Note," *Journal for the Scientific Study of Religion* 18 (1979): 197-98. Additional analysis supporting this conclusion was conducted using the General Social Survey data files: James Allan Davis and Tom W. Smith, *General Social Surveys, 1972-1988* [machine-readable data file] (Chicago: National Opinion Research Center, 1988).

4. Lyle E. Schaller, *Assimilating New Members* (Nashville: Abingdon Press, 1978), 58-59.

5. Douglas W. Johnson, *Vitality Means Church Growth* (Nashville: Abingdon Press, 1989), 56.

6. Ibid., 58.

7. Schaller, *Assimilating New Members*, 52.

8. Schaller, *Growing Plans*, 74.

8
Assimilating, Retaining, and Reclaiming Members

The relationship of a member to his or her church is much like a marriage, except that the decision to break off or continue the relationship rests primarily in the hands of only one party. Using this perspective, the assimilation process can be seen as the engagement. A commitment has been made, but the parties involved are still "checking each other out" to see if the arrangement will become permanent. In the marriage phase the member has become part of the congregation to some degree, and intends to make the relationship work. As in marriage, however, there is the possibility of separation and divorce. People get mad and leave their churches; others drift away and are never seen again; while still others leave in search of something their current church lacks.

Churches tend to place a great deal of emphasis on attracting visitors and recruiting members, but relatively little emphasis on what happens after a person joins. Typically, there are mechanisms for assimilation in place, such as Sunday School, but rarely is there an assessment of the effectiveness of such mechanisms or routine procedures for monitoring how many are leaving "out the back door" and why. If members leave, it is assumed that the relationship simply "did not take," that they found a church which met their needs better, or that their level of commitment to the church was too low to sustain active involvement over the long haul. Organized procedures for *reclaiming* members who drop out are even rarer than are procedures designed to prevent people from leaving the church.

Churches cannot afford to ignore any one of the three issues covered in this chapter. Assimilation, retention, and reclamation are all too important to the growth and vitality of individual churches, and also to the larger family of God as individual congregations seek to reach people for Christ and incorporate them into loving fellowships of believers.

Assimilation

The most frequent response to the question, "why did you join this church?" is, "the people seemed friendly." Of the many things people expect from a church, the possibility of forming relatively close relationships with other members apparently is one of the most important. It should be added, however, that this possibility is seen as a minimum level of acceptability to most Christians. That is, people *expect* churches to be friendly, and they will not consider joining one which is not. Friendliness is, therefore, not a special quality which a few exceptional (and rapidly growing) churches have, it is a quality which most Americans assume churches should possess.

Most congregations *think* they are friendly, and in fact most are, in one way or another. For instance, strong relationships normally exist among the long-term members of any congregation. They have their squabbles, but the core group is much like an extended family. There is love and sometimes even hate, but beneath it all there is a sense of "connectedness," of relationship, which can be distinguished from friendship. If an interviewer were to ask one of these members if the church is friendly, chances are they would say "yes, these are the nicest folk you have ever met, in fact, they are like my family." Unfortunately, these individuals who are so friendly *to one another* may not be friendly at all to newcomers in the congregation. In the worst examples, visitors will be largely ignored and for this reason most will never consider joining such a congregation. More frequently, newcomers will receive a warm welcome, and some will join on the basis of this welcome, fully expecting that they will become part of the fellowship. After a year or two they find that they are no more a part of the church than when they first joined. In fact, they are somewhat worse off, because at least when they were newcomers, someone paid some attention to them. Now they are taken for granted and ignored, except for the expression of meaningless pleasantries. "Hey there, how are you? Kids OK, too?"

The assimilation problem, which all churches exhibit to some degree, has sociological roots. Social groups form *boundaries* which tend to become rigid over time, especially when the group does not experience a regular turnover in its membership. In any social group there is a distinction between us and them—those who have been accepted as part of the group and those who remain outside. These boundaries, which include feelings of us *versus* them, subtle behavioral norms which are unspoken but understood, mutually reinforcing friendship ties, memories of shared experiences, and the sense that "I have in this group all the friends I need" can become very strong and eventually preclude the acceptance of new members. This is particularly true when no institutional mechanism exists for keeping the group open to newcomers, and when the length of membership is completely open-ended.

College fraternities, which also are voluntary associations, have definite boundaries which are reinforced by such things as shared knowledge of what my fellow brothers called "mystic goodies," secret handshakes, frequent fellowships (parties), shared living quarters on many campuses, and so forth. Unlike churches, however, fraternities have an annual rush class, which is an institutional mechanism for incorporating new members, and they also have regular turnover in their membership as seniors graduate. Membership may be viewed as for life, death may be called "the chapter eternal," and despite the efforts of students to prolong their college careers for six, seven, or eight years, fraternities do not have the problem of entrenched members who become so accustomed to each other over the decades that they cannot accept anyone new.

In *small churches,* assimilation is like an adoption—but adoption by a family which thinks it probably has enough children already. Prospective sons or daughters are scrutinized carefully, poked and prodded in order to see if they are "our kind of folks." Newcomers are free to worship in the church, of course, but acceptance is similar to joining an exclusive social club. The club not the applicant decides who is allowed to join.

For *larger churches* which have made the difficult transition from a large family to a multicelled organism composed of many groups, the problem is that the small groups (rather than the church as a whole) tend to become rigid and will not accept newcomers. Without open groups a church lacks what Lyle Schaller calls "points of entry" which allow a new member to begin forming friendship ties with other church members.[1] All large churches have a certain number of "unconnected members" who can be satisfied with quietly listening and learning, but most people want to participate and to establish relationships with others in the church.

These factors are the major reasons why newer churches tend to grow much faster on average than older congregations. In new churches the walls or boundaries which form around social groups have not had time to become rigid. New members gain ready acceptance because in a real sense everyone is a new member. No one grew up in the church. No one has relationships with others that are more than a few years old, and the church still has mission rather than maintenance as its reason for existence. Reaching people is normally a major part of this mission and that implies accepting new people.

As mentioned previously, research has shown that in growing churches members have fewer friends on average within the congregation and tend to want more friends than do the members of nongrowing churches. In nongrowing churches people have many friends, and they do not feel the need for any more.[2] Commitment to the church is high among the members of these churches because so many "redundant ties" bind the individual to the congregation.[3] Unfortunately, the abundance of friends precludes the need for more and newcomers often find that they cannot break into the church. People may be friendly, but they are unavailable as potential friends.

For older churches the task is to make sure that open groups exist and that new members are channeled to these groups. This is essential to church growth. Baptist churches often do this by a rigidly enforced age grading of Sunday School and through the addition of new classes. By limiting the duration that a member spends in a group and by regular promotion of members from department to department or class to class, the church is able to keep (or at least retard) social groups from becoming too rigid and unable to accept newcomers. Since classes receive promotees on an annual basis, accepting new members from outside the church may be easier than in churches which do not make the effort to promote adult Sunday School members.

Churches which use standard age-grading procedures and which divide classes tend to grow. Research results clearly support such a conclusion.[4] Still, there are some drawbacks to these procedure because they may break up the very social groups which members desire in a church. So how does a church have open social groups without undermining their reason for being? The answer appears to be in the formation of *new* groups.

New members should be channeled into new groups whenever possible. For instance, a church which has received several new adult couples should try to start a new Sunday School class for these couples which includes them, a fine teacher, and a few faithful "seed" couples. In such a setting the newcomers will feel immediate acceptance as part of a new venture where they participate in the formation of group boundaries, norms, and relationships. Research findings show that while relatively few churches try to do this on a regular basis, starting new classes for new members is much more characteristic of "breakout churches" than it is of churches which remain on the plateau.[5]

It is also important to get new members involved in a variety of groups, such as task-oriented groups to which they can bring expertise or a new perspective. Since these groups are organized to pursue specific tasks, active participation is more natural and less threatening than in a Sunday School class. Construction workers are able to use their skills in building projects at the church, in service to the community, or in short-term mission trips. Corporate planners and managers make excellent additions to long-range planning task groups. Real estate agents and bankers are excellent additions to task groups which are assigned the job of looking into space needs and property acquisition.

A wide variety of task-oriented groups is possible. Groups can be organized to create Christmas banners for the sanctuary, to hold a special dinner for international students in the community, organize a crisis food pantry, or to do many other tasks. A short-term craft class can serve as a place where long-term members and newcomers can meet and develop relationships on an equal basis. Each group provides the opportunity for assimilation, and the more assimilation opportunities which exist in a church, the likelihood becomes less that a newcomer will "fall through the cracks" and decide that "these people don't really care enough about me and my family to accept us as members."

A final word about assimilation is that new members must be made aware of the possibilities for involvement and be encouraged to participate. This often occurs in new member orientation sessions. As seen in figure 8.1, offering (but not requiring) an orientation for new members is related to church growth, and should be a regular feature in every church—especially in larger congregations, where its relationship with growth is particularly strong.[6]

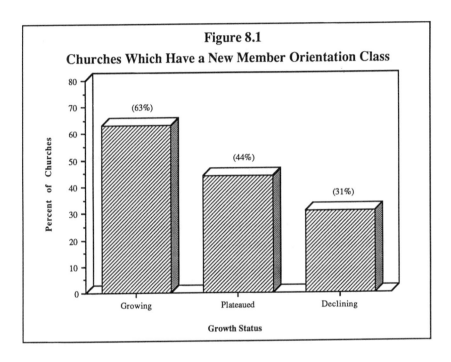

Figure 8.1

Churches Which Have a New Member Orientation Class

Retention

There are three keys to retaining members in a church: (1) keeping members *involved* in activities and relationships; (2) meeting the needs of members; and (3) avoiding making members mad. If a church does these three things well, it will not have to worry much about dropouts, because they will be few.

Keeping members involved is related to assimilation. The more an individual has been absorbed into the life of a church, the less is the likelihood that he or she will *desire* to withdraw, or that the breaking of one important tie within the congregation will sever that key bond which makes participation worthwhile. For many newly active members, however, assimilation has not proceeded far enough to prevent the individual from dropping out if their initial "avenue of entry" turns out to be a blind alley. For instance, the new member may be part of one small group and may only have a few members within that group to call as friends. If such a group is disrupted by dividing the class or by recruiting the new member's only true friends for service elsewhere, the individual may feel that he or she has been left with only casual acquaintances with whom to interact. For this reason, churches should be careful in how they manipulate Sunday School classes, home cell groups, prayer groups, and other vehicles for relationships. Further, care should be taken not to "gut" adult departments of all of their outgoing, committed members. There is a tendency to do this in churches, because such individuals make such effective workers. Unfortunately the unintended consequence of this action is to turn an exciting adult department into one which can only be described as "lifeless." It is impossible to create excitement in such a department because all of the enthusiastic people are serving elsewhere. This not only disillusions members who may view the department as having become barely worthwhile, but it also creates problems in the efforts of the Sunday School to attract new people.

In addition to efforts to avoid the disruption of existing small groups, churches should continually create new opportunities for group involvement. When a task-oriented group is disbanded because its project is over, the new member should be given the opportunity for other types of service or involvement. In growing churches the opportunities are almost endless in number.

Growing churches may have certain program and ministry specialties, but they also tend to have a much wider variety of programs and ministries than do plateaued or declining churches. And each provides opportunities for member involvement. Members who have an idea for a new ministry receive support from the church if such an activity is consistent with the gospel and with the purpose of the congregation. For this reason, research has found greater involvement in social ministries on the part of growing churches than among plateaued and declining congregations, even though there also is a greater tendency toward theological conservatism and an orientation towards evangelism in growing churches.[7] In other words, theological conservatism and an evangelical orientation do not preclude an active program of social ministries. To the contrary, all three can easily coexist and tend to do so in growing Southern Baptist churches. Growing churches typically are vital congregations. They tend to do "both and" rather than "either or." In such settings, new members find a varied array of ministries in which to serve—whatever their interests. The more they become involved in groups related to these ministries, the more ties they create in the church and the less likely they are to consider switching or dropping out.

Research also shows that growing churches keep up with their members better than do plateaued and declining congregations. They are more likely to have a deacon family ministry plan or a zone plan, for instance. As shown in figure 8.2, 75 percent of growing churches have such a plan in operation as compared to 58 percent of plateaued churches and 43 percent of declining congregations. Of course the problems with such efforts are well known to any church which has tried to use them, and modest success is reason for rejoicing. To the degree that these plans are successful in keeping track of *most* of the members of a church and in dealing with a few problems before they get out of hand, a church should count the programs as successful. Because no one program will do all that is necessary to retain members, there is nothing wrong with redundant ministries. What helps one member to feel connected and loved by a congregation may not affect another, but the member unaffected by one program may receive support from an entirely different program.

The second factor in retaining members is meeting their needs. People attend church for a variety of reasons. Caring relationships are one thing that people expect from the church, but they also expect the church to be more than a social club. They expect the church to be religious—to create an environment for worship and for personal growth in faith. If people come to church and week after week hear boring messages, guilt-provoking lectures on social responsibility, incomprehensible theological discourses, and vague sermons with no apparent subject, new members, young adults, and the teenage children of members will begin to wonder about the relevance of the church to their lives. What does God have to do with this church? Is it possible to have an encounter with God in this setting—to see God act and transform lives? Can I grow in my faith in this setting? Can I learn more about God's Word in this environment? Can I get anything from this church which will help me to live a more Christlike life in the world? Is there anything this church is doing which will allow me to express my need to

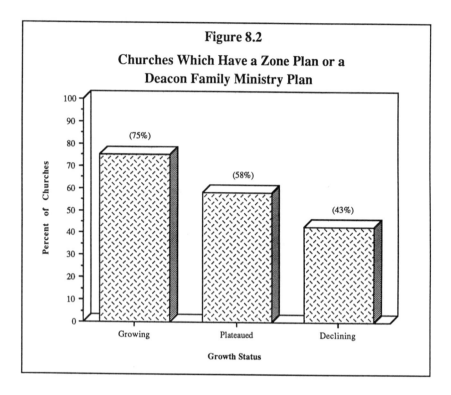

Figure 8.2

Churches Which Have a Zone Plan or a Deacon Family Ministry Plan

minister to others? These are the questions that many Christians are asking today, and many mainline and traditionalistic conservative churches are being found wanting.

Perhaps the largest source of membership loss among Protestant churches today is the drifting away of members—especially the children of members as they become teenagers or young adults. These individuals do not leave in a huff. They go away to college, or they move out of their parent's homes and never find their way back into the church.[9] To prevent this hemorrhage of our lifeblood churches must ensure that there is something within the church for people to commit themselves to.

The third factor in preventing dropouts relates to not making members mad. Research into church dropouts (including those who continue to identify with the church, but who rarely attend) indicates that many are *estranged* from the church.[10] Someone or something made them mad and no one has done anything to alleviate the sense of hurt. The sources of these hurts and "beefs" are varied.

One major source of frustration on the part of active members is overwork. Churches often use and overuse their most committed and effective members. These are people who want to help and do not know how to say "no" when the load becomes too great. Typically they will wait until the end of a big job and then switch to another church with a vow never to accept another assignment. Churches should be aware of the load they give to their most effective lay leaders. They cannot afford to lose them, and overwork is one of the best ways to do so.

Another source of anger is the restrictiveness and judgmental nature of many conservative Protestant and Catholic churches. Baptists and Catholic churches have lost untold thousands of members who left because they felt the church was condemning them rather than their sin, or that it was creating new issues to call sin, as if there were not already enough things which were wrong. This is not to say that churches should relax their moral teachings in order to placate potential dropouts. They should not. However, they should take a close look at what is being condemned and see to what extent the condemnation is based on tradition rather than on Scripture. They should also avoid condemnation of the individual. The emphasis should be positive on what God can do in a person's life, rather than on only judgment.

Yet another source of pain are those truly malicious hurts which are inflicted by unfeeling church members, pastors, and church staff. Although such instances may happen infrequently, they can be so devastating that they are remembered for years and cause many to leave the church. A church in Texas, for instance, which was embroiled in conflict between two warring factions recently threw out one of its more prominent members because the leaders of one faction in the church realized that they had the votes for expulsion. The action nearly destroyed the church. Members on both sides of the conflict left, and the church declined by over 80 percent in membership and attendance during the subsequent three years. Similar devastation often occurs when it comes to light that a pastor or staff member has become involved in immoral or illegal activity. Those who looked up to the accused as a role model feel betrayed and disillusioned. Many leave the church after such an incident and will bring it up to anyone who broaches the subject of the church thereafter.

Finally, there is the perception that church members "just don't care." When they had a need, resulting from a death in the family or an illness, no one came to help. They waited for the church to respond, and when it did not, they left the church, expecting someone to ask "why?" And when no one bothered to ask the question, they became very bitter toward the church. This may be another reason why churches which keep track of their members and where the pastor is heavily involved in counseling are more likely to grow. In such churches there is the perception that people care and that help is available from the pastor in times of crisis (so people will also feel free to ask for help, rather than suffering in silence). There is also less likelihood that someone will "fall through the cracks" and be left out of the caring safety net which so many churches provide to their members in need.

Reclaiming Inactive Members and Dropouts

The pastors of growing congregations were more likely to say that their churches did a good job in reclaiming inactive members than did the pastors of nongrowing churches. This was not unexpected. However, it seems apparent that relatively few churches actually are very effective in this area—even growing congregations. Most of the growing churches said they were only average, whereas plateaued and declining churches tended to rate "below average" in reclaiming inactive members.

How growing churches actually pursue lapsed members is not very clear from survey data. Visiting those who had dropped out of the church was unrelated to church growth, as was the number of times a person had to miss Sunday School before they received a visit. So how are growing churches doing a better job in reclaiming inactives if they are no more likely to be involved in activities designed to reclaim these dropouts? It may be that in the absence of effective *programs* for reclaiming inactives, what may be important is the overall attitude of the congregation. If a church exudes love and acceptance, as so often happens in growing congregations, it may be that contacts with inactives occur naturally and spontaneously, rather than through any sort of organized effort. Inactives soon realize that fellow members want them to return and the decision to reduce participation was due to some aspect of their own life rather than due to something which the church had done. If such is the case, then it would appear that growing churches do a better job in reclaiming inactive members simply by treating all members as valued people to whom the church wishes to minister. It should be pointed out, however, that nearly all churches could do a much better job in keeping track of their members and intervening when people drop out. One way this is being done by many growing churches is through a yearly churchwide visitation of members. This periodic effort to listen to issues on the minds of members and to keep in touch with their needs creates the ongoing sense that the church cares. Such a caring attitude not only helps prevent dropouts, but it may help bring members back—especially younger members who have dropped out while in high school or after leaving for college.

More intensive efforts to visit and counsel dropouts within a few weeks after they reduce participation are not highly correlated with church growth, and such activities certainly are less important than are efforts to deal with sources of disaffection with the church *before* members leave. Intensive efforts to reach drop outs may be worthwhile, however, in terms of making sure that a church does not lose the very persons it is seeking to reach—the unchurched and barely churched. Such individuals are likely to join the church with little commitment and drift away for insignificant reasons. Efforts should be made to draw in these marginal members. They are a growing population in American society and our churches cannot afford to contribute further to their proliferation.

Notes

1. Lyle E. Schaller, *Hey, That's Our Church* (Nashville: Abingdon Press, 1975), 36.

2. Daniel V. A. Olson, "Church Friendships: Boon or Barrier to Church Growth?" *Journal for the Scientific Study of Religion* 28 (1989): 442-43.

3. Lyle E. Schaller, "Redundant Ties," *The Parish Paper* 17:6 (1987): 2.

4. This refers to my study of church growth among 543 growing, plateaued, and declining metropolitan Southern Baptist churches.

5. This research is from my survey comparing "breakout churches" with churches remaining on statistical plateaus. The survey was conducted among Southern Baptist churches in 1988.

6. A question regarding a required new member training class was asked on the church on the plateau survey. Having such a class is associated with breakout growth, but the relationship is quite weak and does not reach an acceptable level of statistical significance.

7. Findings from both the general church growth survey and the church on the plateau survey indicated that growing churches and breakout churches were more involved in ministry to the community and had a wider range of ministries in operation than did plateaued or declining churches. In addition, research among churches with effective Christian education programs suggests that vital churches tend to have both social ministry and outreach, rather than one or the other. Also see Douglas W. Johnson, *Vitality Means Church Growth* (Nashville: Abingdon Press, 1989), 95-102.

8. See Lyle E. Schaller, "A Second Look at the Zone Plan," *The Parish Paper* 9:2 (1979): 1-2.

9. See C. Kirk Hadaway, *What Can We Do About Church Dropouts?* (Nashville: Abingdon Press, 1990).

10. Ibid., chapters 2 and 3.

9

Innovation and Distinctiveness

Growth is a form of change. It involves incorporating new people, creating new groups, developing an increasingly complex organizational structure, adding new staff, and often the construction of expanded facilities. Growth includes change in the form of *adding things*, but it also comes in the form of *giving things up*—some of which have become very comfortable.

Sunday School class members may be called upon to give up a cherished classroom; a growing church may find it necessary to relocate from a historic structure to a new location which has no history; long-term members may lose their right to have the ultimate "say so" in important decisions; deacons may have to exchange their role as a board of directors for that of a ministering body; the style of worship may have to change to accommodate new residents; and the pastor may become less available to members as time demands grow in a larger church. In general, people in the church (and everywhere else) want to have their cake and eat it too. Which is to say that people want to have the good things that come from growth, but they would prefer to avoid giving up other good things which are characteristic of smaller congregations. Since this is impossible, the growing church walks a tenuous trail on which members must be prodded forward by assurances that the changes which growth inevitably brings are worthwhile. Resistance to change is natural and should be expected by any pastor or task force which is attempting to create a new vision for growth, to organize a growth strategy, or to formulate a new ministry.

Some churches have a more serious problem in this area than do others, however. For instance, older churches are much more likely to resist change than are younger congregations. Older churches have fulfilled their initial mission and find it difficult to develop a new role and new goals. Further, they tend to be dominated by older members who have been leaders in the church for many years—people who have seen programs come and go, who have experienced the efforts of a succession of pastors to either revitalize the church or "go with the flow," and who feel that they have earned their right to have a comfortable church which has been structured to suit them and their friends.

Rural churches, village churches, and small churches in stable, older neighborhoods are also more likely to resist change. Limited resources and the belief that growth is extremely unlikely in their setting have led the "congregation's governing body to drift into a permission withholding stance when ideas for new ministries and new programs are proposed."[1] As Lyle Schaller notes, "this posture tends to inhibit the creativity of the members, to halt the flow of innovative suggestions from individuals and program committees and to encourage passivity."[2] Maintaining the current institutional structure, staff, and ministries is seen as difficult enough, and church leaders cannot imagine doing anything *beyond* what they do now because they can barely make ends meet as it is.

Large, highly institutionalized, denominationally oriented churches with long-tenured pastors also are highly resistant to change. They have become church versions of calcified bureaucracies. These churches are not passive in the sense that they fulfilled their original goals and became directionless.[3] They are purposefully passive. In their self-satisfied role as guardians of the faith and tradition, they maintain each program which the denomination suggests, support cooperative giving to denominational causes without question, and hold worship services which are objectively excellent, if not particularly exciting. There is no felt need for change in such congregations, because there is the definite sense that they got it right the first time—so why change? The fact that these churches are invariably on the plateau is either ignored as irrelevant or explained away by references to demographic problems.

Even though all churches tend to resist change to some degree, there are certain types of congregations where change is less of a problem. One of these is the newer church. New churches are in the process of becoming something—a fact which is recognized and accepted by members. They see this thing they are moving toward as a possibility, as a dreamed-for goal, but as something which has not yet come to pass. To achieve this goal, members recognize that change is inevitable and will be relatively constant for years to come. The goal may involve achieving a certain degree of stability and comfort, but until the church is successful in attracting enough members to consider calling a full-time pastor, until they are able to afford to build a permanent facility, and until they are able to add that educational wing, stability and comfort are not really expected.

The other type of church where change is less of a problem is the very purposeful congregation which has a long history of growth. Some churches have been able to institutionalize the need for change. Their goal is to reach people for Christ, and if they are successful in this endeavor they will grow. Growth causes the need for more of everything—space, staff, and organization. These are accepted as inevitable and the continuing need to change reinforces the image of the church as successful in achieving its ongoing purpose. There is the temptation for these churches to rest, to reach a point where members say "this is as big as we need to get," but if the goal of reaching others is clearly in place, the pastor can easily overcome the natural longing for stability through reference to the shared vision which has fueled the growth of the church for so long.

The Necessity for Change in Nongrowing Churches

For churches which are not growing, business as usual will only lead to the continuation of current trends. Plateaued and declining congregations are unlikely to achieve renewed growth unless major changes are made in their self-image, orientation, and actions—except in those rare cases where unexpected population growth bring a flood of newcomers who transform a church by the force of their numbers, their new ideas, and their enthusiasm. Of course, the problem is that members in many churches do not want to change, only want nondisruptive changes, or their desire for change is very passive.

Breakout churches and growing churches, in general, are characterized by a greater openness to innovation and by a greater willingness to change than is likely to be found among plateaued and declining congregations. As can be seen in figure 9.1, growing congregations tend to be rated as more "innovative" than "traditional." In an earlier chapter it was also seen that growing congregations are more likely to "dream about the future" rather than "live in the past" (see fig. 5.1). Similarly, in figure 9.2, it is clear that breakout churches are much more likely to have experienced an increased "willingness to change" than are churches which remain on statistical plateaus.

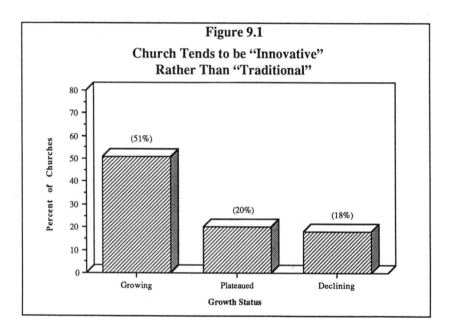

Figure 9.1

Church Tends to be "Innovative" Rather Than "Traditional"

Interviews with pastors of breakout churches also underscored the importance of openness to change. Although in most cases the willingness to change had to be awakened to some degree (or at least energized by a renewed vision for growth), breakout growth was much easier and came much faster if the members of the church had already determined that change was a necessity if the church was to grow or to begin moving toward definite objectives.

In contrast to breakout churches, many plateaued congregations are very traditionalistic and are antichange in orientation. Members become very upset when someone attempts to alter the order of worship, the Sunday School curriculum, the time of the worship service, the number of worship services, the style of hymns, the version of the Bible used in worship, and so forth. The wife of a pastor friend was even reminded by a church member that they expected their pastor to wear white shirts when he preached. These things and many others are sacred in traditionalistic congregations.

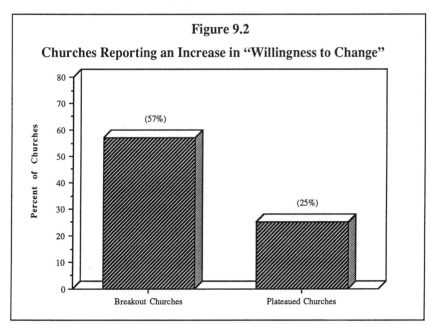

Figure 9.2

Churches Reporting an Increase in "Willingness to Change"

Of course, no congregation is homogeneous in the orientation of its members toward change. Peter Wagner notes, "the people of your congregation will fall along a spectrum from radicals through progressives and conservatives to traditionalists at the other extreme."[4] Even so, each church also will exhibit a *general orientation toward change*. For churches where there is a general openness to change, it will be much easier for a new pastor or for a long-tenured pastor with new ideas to institute the changes necessary for renewed growth.

Many things contribute to this orientation toward change. In a church in southern Kentucky, the elderly members were so afraid that their generation was going to be the last in the church that they were willing to put aside their need for comfort and stability and accept the necessity for change in the form of evangelism and growth. They allowed a new pastor to lead them in this direction, almost from the day of his arrival.

In several other churches, many of the members were tired of going nowhere, of being a "dead church" and were thankfully willing to follow a stable, effective pastor when one was finally called to the church. In another "breakout church" most members were not particularly excited about the prospect of growth and change, but they did not actively resist the pastor's initial efforts to revitalize the congregation. In the words of the new pastor, "they were passively for growth." This passive openness allowed the pastor to introduce small changes, which then led to support for more sweeping changes once members began to "catch the vision" which the pastor was preaching, teaching, and living out.

Churches which have experienced breakout growth on the order of 50 percent or more over a four-year period have all been characterized by either an openness to change or at least by the passive permission for limited change. As yet, no dramatic examples of breakout growth have been found among churches which were very resistant to change. It is likely that breakout growth, if it can to occur at all in such churches, would take longer to initiate and would be somewhat less dramatic than would be the case in congregations which were open to change.

If a church already has a positive orientation to growth and change, it is the role of the pastor to lead the congregation toward the proper actions which will result in growth. In smaller churches this may mean reviving evangelistic visitation through the efforts of the pastor and a few lay followers. In larger churches the process is likely to be much more complicated, involving long-range planning committees, the formulation of a new purpose statement, formal goal setting, organized church-growth campaigns, and other such activities. In any church which is receptive to growth, the changes should begin as soon as possible before the siren song of comfort is heeded by unwary members and convinces them to relax. The effort should be to introduce enough change so that the church will begin to grow, but not enough as to create serious conflicts within the congregation. If these actions produce growth they will provide some of the legitimation for additional changes. As one member notes, "you can't argue with success."

The necessity for change must be rooted in a sense of purpose which has been accepted or which is *being developed* by the members of a congregation. No one wants change for the sake of change. For churches which are willing to change, the effort should be to fan the flame which gave rise to the initial openness and to provide additional motivation for change—in the form of a renewed vision for the future of the church. For churches which see no need for change, a longer educational process is necessary in order to show members what the church can become. In either case, by allowing members to be part of the envisioning process, the new, hoped-for purpose of the church is more likely to be believed, accepted, and owned. This naturally reinforces any willingness to change which may exist, and it motivates members to work toward the fulfillment of their shared vision.

Distinctiveness and Specialties

Church-growth writers and church practitioners are nearly unanimous in their advice to churches to focus on a small number of specialties, rather than trying to do everything well. According to Schaller, growing churches have a definite image in the community which is based on what they do best. People say, " 'That's the church with the great youth program.' 'That's the church with a strong adult educational program.' 'They have the best music program in town.' "[5] This message is echoed by Kennon Callahan, "a church that has successfully developed a major program that meets community's standard in that specific field of endeavor earns community-wide respect for that program. Effective congregations tend to have at least one major program that is held in high esteem by the community as a whole. The program could be the music program, the youth program, the mother's morning out program . . . the list could go on and on."[6]

Research into the issue of distinctiveness gives some insight into the nature of its relationship to congregational vitality and growth, but the results remain somewhat unequivocal. First of all, growing churches do view themselves as distinctive. Eighty-nine percent of growing church pastors said "yes" to the question "is it easy to describe for visitors how your congregation differs from other congregations in the area?" as compared to 66 percent of the pastors in both plateaued and declining churches. Similar results were obtained when breakout churches were compared to churches which remained on the plateau. This was not surprising. As many observers have noted, there is something tangibly different about growing churches. They are distinctive. Members know it and visitors sense it. This difference may be difficult to articulate, but it seems very real.

The question remains, of course, as to whether having distinctive *programs* helps create the sense of distinctiveness in a congregation which in turn leads to vitality, to a heightened community presence, and, finally, to growth. Unfortunately, research does not provide a clear answer to this question, but there is some evidence that distinctive programs are not a *major* source of church growth. In a survey which compared churches which had grown off the plateau to churches which remained on the plateau it was found that 46 percent of breakout churches responded that they had specialized ministries for which they were well known, as compared to 35 percent of churches remaining on the plateau. The difference was small and not statistically significant.

Growing churches are slightly more likely to have a few "specialties" for which they are well known. Having a specialty is rarely a *key* to growth, however, except in a few growing churches which are properly called "special purpose churches." Such congregations fill certain ministry niches in large urban areas. These churches are known for one unusual thing and count on that thing to draw people from a wide area. Examples include congregations organized to reach small ethnic populations, such as an Iranian Baptist mission in Nashville, Tennessee. Atlanta, Georgia, supports several unusual special-purpose churches. One is a Southern Baptist congregation known for its rather high-church liturgy. Another church has a very active social ministry program—especially in the area of world hunger. Other examples of special-purpose churches around the nation include congregations known for healing ministries, for charismatic worship, for their racial mixture, and for social activism. These churches are distinctive because of their specialties and some are growing (though not all).

Most growing churches are not special-purpose congregations, and the pastors of most growing congregations are hard-pressed to identify one or two things that their church does very well. Instead, these pastors say "we try to do the basics—and we work hard at them." In other words, growing church pastors believe that growth occurs by doing effective evangelism and outreach, by organizing a good working Sunday School, by holding exciting worship services, and by cultivating a sense of warmth and purpose. They may have specialities which help support these basics, but without the basics the church would not see any growth in their opinion. In fact, these pastors often criticize other churches because they only seem to play at the basics, while growing churches really work at them.

It also is true that many growing churches are characterized more by the sheer *variety* of programs than by the exceptional nature of one or two ministries. In such cases, the distinctive feature of the church may be that they do *everything*. If a member wants to be involved in evangelism, they have Evangelism Explosion and an active Sunday School visitation program. If a member is interested in teaching, the church runs two Sunday Schools, has weekly training sessions for teachers, and takes Christian education very seriously. If a member is interested in social ministry, the church has a clothes closet and an emergency food pantry, relates to other crisis counseling ministries, holds conversational English classes, and has a literacy training program. The list goes on and on. Some growing churches have a wider variety of ministries than others (in some the list is amazingly long), but growing churches, in general, tend to have more ministries than nongrowing churches which are of a similar size. Growing churches are vital, and this vitality is often expressed more in the sheer number of ministries than in the exceptional nature of one or two ministries.

The distinctiveness of most growing churches apparently results from a number of factors, rather than because they are exceptional in an area of ministry. First of all, growing churches have direction. The church is on a mission, and members tend to be excited about and supportive of the role or purpose of their church. Second, growing churches are exciting places. Not only does worship tend to be more "celebrative" and "expectant" than it is in nongrowing churches, there is general sense that "something is happening here." God is clearly at work, and He has blessed this church and its ministry. Third, growing churches are warm and welcoming. This is sensed by visitors, and it is interpreted as friendliness by members when they are asked what makes their church different. They say "it is a very friendly church. I felt it when I first visited, and I feel it now." Fourth, there is a sense that the church is ready to try anything new if it will help the congregation reach people for Christ and minister to those in need. The focus is on providing a way to do as much as they can, using the talents and interests of members, rather than on limiting programs and ministries to what the church can afford under its current budget. All these things contribute to the sense of distinctiveness, to the sense that this church is unusual.

What About Denominational Distinctiveness?

The rise of large, independent churches across America and the tendency of some denominational churches to downplay their denominational identity has led to the question of whether a denominational connection is a help or a hindrance to a church in its efforts to grow. This is a sensitive issue among denominational churches and there clearly is not an easy answer to whether or not the connection helps or hurts. Much depends on where a church is located and who it is trying to reach.

A Southern Baptist church in the South might have little reason to fear using the term "Baptist" in its name. Outside the South, however, numerous Southern Baptist churches have dropped (or never added) the word *Baptist* to their names, while others have chosen not to use *Southern*. These churches tend to remain supportive of denominational programs, but they fear that a clear identification with the Southern Baptist Convention might scare potential members or limit their ability to reach unchurched persons who might view Southern Baptists as backwoods snake handlers, bombastic Bible thumpers, or small-minded racists. For this reason in the Los Angeles area there is a Saddleback Valley Community Church, a Church on Brady, and quite a few other Southern Baptist congregations which identify themselves by their location but not by their denominational affiliation. At the same time, however, Los Angeles is home to another church which calls itself the Old Fashioned Southern Baptist Church.

There is no data available regarding whether the use of Baptist in a name helps or hinders church growth. It is likely that those Southern Baptist churches in California which have dropped the word *Baptist* are growing faster than those which have retained it. However, it is unclear to what extent the age of congregation and the general mission orientation of the congregation would explain the possible growth differential rather than the lack of a Baptist label. Nevertheless, two church-growth surveys did ask whether "your church has a strong sense of its Baptist identity?" The vast majority of pastors responded "yes" to this question, but growing church pastors and the pastors of breakout churches were slightly more likely to say "no." Eighty eight percent of breakout church pastors said their church had a strong sense of its Baptist identity, as compared to 96 percent of pastors of churches which remained on the plateau. The relationship was small and not statistically significant, but its direction was the same in two separate church-growth surveys.

In another study, which involved surveys of over eleven thousand church members in six denominations it was found that denominational loyalty among the members of a congregation was unrelated to church growth.[7] These findings support a conclusion that denominational identity is almost irrelevant to the growth of an individual congregation. Many other factors simply are much more important.

Notes

1. Lyle E. Schaller, *Activating the Passive Church* (Nashville: Abingdon Press, 1981), 48.

2. Ibid.

3. Ibid., 51-66.

4. C. Peter Wagner, *Leading Your Church to Growth*, rev. ed. (Ventura, Calif.: Regal Books, 1984), 196.

5. Lyle E. Schaller, *Growing Pains* (Nashville: Abingdon Press, 1983), 66.

6. Kennon Callahan, *Twelve Keys to an Effective Church* (New York: Harper and Row, 1983), 65.

7. Average scores in denominational loyalty produced a .07 Pearson's correlation with church growth in a combined data set of over five hundred churches. This correlation was insignificant. Churches were drawn randomly for this study of effective Christian education from six denominations, which included the Christian Church (Disciples of Christ), Evangelical Lutheran Church in America, the Presbyterian Church (USA), the Southern Baptist Convention, the United Church of Christ, and the United Methodist Church. The study was conducted by Search Institute and was partially funded by the Lilly Endowment, Inc.

10
Spirituality and Ministry

There is a tendency in some circles to view growing churches as somehow tainted, as if their growth could only have come through a single-minded concern for numbers, through gimmicks and huckster-ism, or through the efforts of a manipulative "super preacher" with the ability to draw a crowd and "close a sale." Unfortunately, such stereo-types are often reinforced by real-life examples. There are many pastors for whom evangelism and church growth supersede the need for any other goals, such as one pastor who remarked, "If someone has a problem, I have two minutes to spend with him; my time is reserved for reaching the lost."[1] There are other churches which promote Sunday School by giving away goldfish or twelve apostles charm bracelets. Similarly, it has been impossible to ignore the rise of so many pastor-evangelists (on television and elsewhere) who are apparently blessed with the spiritual gift of crowd manipulation.

Despite the high profile of so many bad examples which serve to reinforce negative stereotypes about growing congregations, there is clear evidence that growing churches are more likely to be "well rounded" in their character and in their array of programs than are churches which are not experiencing growth. In this chapter, two of these areas of "well roundedness" are addressed: spirituality and ministry to the community.

Spirituality

In a recent meeting of Baptist Sunday School Board and Home Mission Board leaders dealing the issue of church growth, Charles Chaney remarked that if he were to revise his well-known book, *Design for Church Growth,* the one key church-growth principle he would add would be *prayer.*[2] For Chaney, Peter Wagner, and many other writers in the church-growth tradition, there is an increasing recognition of the important role played by prayer and by the overall spiritual maturity of a congregation on church growth.

Growing congregations are not only evangelistic and outreach oriented. They also place a greater emphasis on prayer, and most appear to make the spiritual growth of their members a major priority. For instance, survey results seen in figure 10.1 show that 63 percent of breakout churches are rated by their pastors as "excellent" or "good" in the spiritual growth of their members as compared to only 34 percent of churches which continue on the plateau. Also, results from a major study of effective Christian education conducted among six denominations (five mainline Protestant and the Southern Baptist Convention) have shown that churches characterized a greater emphasis on spiritual development in their adult Christian education program also tend to be growing congregations.[3]

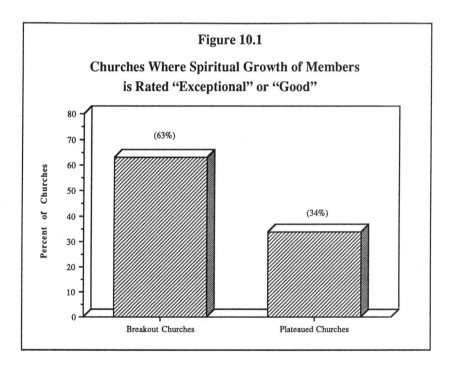

Figure 10.1

Churches Where Spiritual Growth of Members is Rated "Exceptional" or "Good"

It is not enough for a church to want growth, to plan for growth, to have an enthusiastic pastor who is trying to lead the church to grow, or to institute the proper programs which are designed to achieve growth. Renewal must occur within the congregation. The church must be lifted to a higher plane in terms of confidence, commitment, and faith. It must develop a new spirit.

Part of this new spirit involves a reorientation of congregational priorities. Prayer can play a major part in this reorientation by focusing members' eyes on the true purpose of the church. As Bill Sullivan notes, "prayer changes people. [It] inevitably brings us to realize that God wants us to reach the lost, to find people who are outside the fold."[4] So, even if we ignore the supernatural power that is available through prayer and the willingness of God to bless a congregation which turns to Him, a renewed prayer ministry can have very tangible benefits for an aimless congregation. Among other things, it can lead to a greater openness to evangelism and outreach, which are major correlates of church growth. It may also lead to a greater concern for those in need. In short, by changing people, prayer can help a church become well rounded and vital. Such a church almost always experiences growth, unless it is in an area where growth is demographically impossible.

Prayer also can produce *a receptive climate for change.* It fixes the attention of members on what is important to God, on the needs of church members, and on needs which exist in the community. Through earnest prayer, members may come to realize what God expects of their church, and that by contrast, the maintenance goals, the petty squabbles, and the power struggles which are a part of most aimless churches seem insignificant. The commitment of church members to ministry comes to outweigh the need for comfort, and members become receptive to changes designed to accomplish what God expects of the church.

Survey results underscore the important role of a prayer ministry in a congregation. As can be seen in figure 10.2, *71 percent* of breakout churches report an increased emphasis on prayer over the past several years as compared to only 40 percent of churches which continue on the plateau. This rather large difference indicates that one part of the revitalization which has taken place in breakout churches came in the form of a renewed emphasis on prayer.

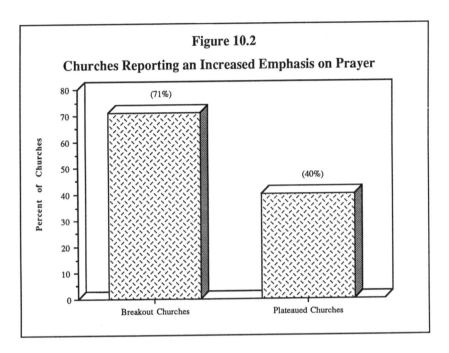

Figure 10.2

Churches Reporting an Increased Emphasis on Prayer

As a church devotes more energy to the spiritual development of its members, several things begin to happen. First, members become ministers and thus become able to use their spiritual gifts to help the church grow. They not only minister through *existing* programs of the church, they also seek *new ways* to minister to others. They get involved. They organize prayer groups and Bible studies on their own initiative. They witness to their friends about Christ and they invite them to church. They become more sensitive to those around them who are hurting and try to find ways that they can help.

Another thing which happens to a church as its members become stronger Christians is that the congregation becomes more willing to step out on faith—to trust God to provide, even when something does not seem possible in the light of past failures. This is an essential change for a congregation that wishes to grow off the plateau. As seen earlier, growing churches set goals for themselves, and these goals must be challenging if they are to inspire members to act. But before members are willing to set challenging goals for themselves they must have some sense that God is with them in this endeavor—that God will help them achieve the goal. This is unlikely in a congregation which neglects the spiritual maturity of its members. However, in churches where members have seen God act through transforming lives through and answered prayer, there is a much greater likelihood that members will trust God to act again. They are willing to attempt great things for God, because they know that God honors the expression of faith.

Millions of Christians want spiritual depth in their lives and they are not finding a way to grow in many mainline and conservative churches in America. People are seeking churches which can provide an opportunity for spiritual growth, and when one exists, the word spreads quickly and people are drawn like bees to honey. "At last," members say, "I will not have to go outside my own congregation for the type of in-depth Bible study and prayer which I need." The void created by the lack of such churches has led to the development of many parachurch organizations which are designed to provide intensive Bible study and (or) a setting for intercessory prayer.

In some churches the strong Christian is a source of threat to the pastor and minister of education. Such people are always wanting to know why we do it this way, why we use this literature, and whether or not we can try this new ministry or program. However, in many growing churches, the strong Christian is a valued resource, who can be used to start and staff new ministries which might be beyond the comfort level of most members. With many such members, and a constant supply of new ones, a church can continually expand its outreach and ministry—without the necessity of adding paid staff.

Ministry to the Community

Churches in growing conservative denominations have been criticized for their apparent myopic concern with evangelism and church growth. They have been accused of ignoring the words of Jesus to care for the poor and to minister to those in need. On the other hand, mainline churches have been criticized by their conservative "cousins" for being overly concerned with social issues—with changing the world—and by doing so they have failed to offer the good news of Christ to those who need it most.

There is some truth in each of these criticisms, of course. In some conservative churches, growth is the primary concern of the pastor and staff. Other functions of a vital New Testament church are either ignored or given slight attention. Conversely, many mainline churches do seem to ignore outreach. They say they are open to all—especially to marginal members of society which many churches ignore—but they fail to reach out to these people and invite them into their congregations.

From a "hard-nosed" church-growth perspective, the question is not whether social action and social ministry are things churches should do, regardless of their impact on growth. The question is whether or not they are positively or negatively related to the growth of congregations. This is not an easy question to answer.

Previous research in this area has suggested that social ministry *per se* does not work against the growth of a congregation. However, when social ministry is couched in terms of certain types of social activism or when it becomes clear that the primary emphasis of a congregation is on social change, then we begin to see negative relationships with church growth—at least within samples composed primarily of white churches. For instance, a study of church growth conducted among United Presbyterian congregations in the 1970s revealed that questions dealing with the importance of trying to change society (asked to both the pastor and for members) produced negative relationships with growth.[5] In other words, churches where the pastor put great importance on trying to change society were more likely to be *declining* than were churches where the pastor placed less importance on such a goal. On the other hand, this same survey showed that involvement in the community and even activities like helping to organize disadvantaged groups in the community to petition their grievances were positively associated with church growth.

These findings should not be taken to imply that working to change the structural sources of social injustice leads churches to decline, and therefore should be avoided by churches that wish to grow. Many predominantly African-American churches are heavily involved in efforts to change society and many of these churches are growing rapidly. In fact, the pastor of a rapidly growing African-American Southern Baptist church in Chicago credits at least part of the growth of his congregation to various social programs—including lobbying, marching and boycotting. Social activism *per se* does not lead churches to decline. Instead, it is the constellation of other characteristics typical of the white, social-activist church which leads to decline. If white congregations could disassociate social activism from its theologically liberal, non-evangelistic, upper-class, intellectual connotations, the negative relationship probably would not exist.

In a survey of Southern Baptist churches which compared breakout churches to churches which remained on the plateau, questions were not asked about *social activism*, but there were several questions dealing with ministry to the community. As in the Presbyterian survey, responses to these questions clearly indicated that ministry to the community was associated with church growth. For instance, on the question, "How involved is your church in providing ministry to the surrounding community?" 37 percent of the breakout churches were involved "to a large extent," as compared to only 17 percent of the continued plateau churches. This relationship is shown graphically in figure 10.3. Similar associations, although slightly weaker, were found for

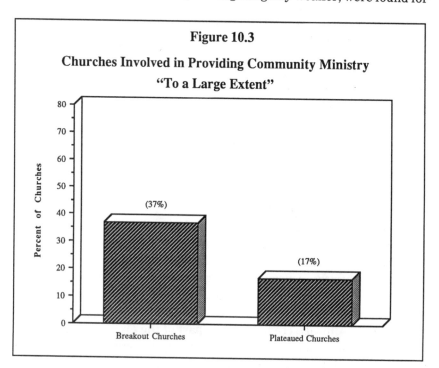

Figure 10.3

**Churches Involved in Providing Community Ministry
"To a Large Extent"**

a question dealing with increased or decreased emphasis on "ministry to the community" over the past several years.

We do not know, of course, exactly what each pastor means by "ministry to the community." However, it is clear that breakout churches (and growing churches generally) tend to have a greater *presence* in their community. They are less inward looking and see the role of the church as helping people, whether they are members of the congregation or not. As a result, persons in the community are aware that the church exists and that it is available in time of need. The goals of providing ministry to the community were not designed to produce growth in these churches, but it would appear that growth can be an unintended consequence. The ministering church is seen as an open, accepting congregation, rather than as a restricted social club. Further, those who have received help or support and those on the outside who have worked on joint ministry projects with the church may establish relationships with the pastor or members, come to know Christ (if they do not already), and eventually join the fellowship.

In one growing congregation, the pastor was called upon to perform the funeral of a teenager from the local high school, who had been killed in an auto accident. Although the student was not a member of the church, he had come to know the pastor. During the funeral the church played a song by a popular rock group which meant a great deal to the student. This simple act, which many would have seen as inappropriate for a church, much less for a funeral, made a great impression on many students from the community and on their unchurched parents. After the funeral a woman came up to the pastor, and said "I have never had any use for the church, but I would like to be able to call you if my family ever experiences a crisis." Of course the pastor said that he would be happy to respond. This was only one of many opportunities for ministry *and* outreach which came out of an effort to be sensitive to the needs of others.

While some growing churches are exclusively concerned with growth, the majority of growing congregations are well-rounded churches which are doing ministry as well as evangelism. They are what Douglas Johnson calls "vital churches." He goes on to say, "involvement in the community is a hallmark of vital churches. This involvement finds various ways of expressing itself so that, as one keeps following leads, a network of people and money is created to help work at solving community problems as well as meeting human needs. . . . Witnessing through service is a normal part of ministry as taught in these churches."[6] Also according to Johnson, the community programs in which vital congregations were active included "food and clothing banks, job or employment reference centers, referral centers for people needing a place to live, child and women abuse clinics, community health screening programs, and Habitat for Humanity."[7]

Some vital congregations become so involved in creating new ministries that they even "give them away" to the community when social service agencies recognize their value or when they outgrow the resources of the church. Allen Temple Baptist Church in Oakland, California, is one example of a church that has done this on a regular basis. Members with a ministry idea are given the full support of the church, although the members are expected to "carry the ball." When such ministries "take off," as several have, such as the health clinic, they often become too large for the church and too valuable to the community for the church to maintain control. By giving up these ministries, it becomes possible for them to grow further through government grants and other fund-raising activities which a church connection might hurt.

Ministry and Pluralism

The ability of a church to be involved in ministry to its community is often determined by the social character of the congregation, rather than by the willingness of members to be involved. A church which is drawn from its surrounding community will stand a much better chance for ministry and for growth than a congregation which has slowly become different from the population of its surrounding neighborhoods. Since communities change, it is necessary for churches to change along with their communities.

Unfortunately, it is difficult for most churches to change in composition because they were organized as "homogeneous units." There is a widespread myth propagated by the church-growth school of thought that homogeneous congregations grow faster than pluralistic congregations. This is an ideological position which is unsupported by research of any kind—except that dealing with tribal societies outside the American context. The fact is, the majority of churches in America, growing, plateaued, and declining are homogeneous, and there is no evidence which suggests that higher degrees of homogeneity are correlated with higher levels of growth. Further, efforts to find churches which are self-consciously using the homogeneous-unit principle (directing outreach efforts only at those "like us") have been futile. Too few churches are doing so (except for ethnic congregations) for any kind of a test of the homogeneous-unit principle in the American context. It remains an un-tested proposition, which has been made to seem credible by the fact that most growing congregations are homogeneous and by the efforts of church-growth apologists to find some elusive basis of homogeneity in even the most heterogeneous growing congregations.

There are many ways for a church to structure racial, ethnic, income, and life-style diversity within itself through the existence of homoge-neous subgroups in the congregation and through "a pluralistic style of ministry and a varied and diverse program."[8] Case studies of churches with effective Christian education programs revealed many *growing churches* with great diversity—which was a source of great pride in all denominations (conservative and mainline). Just as growing churches are typically open to forming new community ministries, the openness of such congregations tends to attract a variety of people, many of whom do not fit the dominant character of the congregation. In some cases these individuals may coalesce to form a Sunday School class or fellowship group of their own, but in other cases the church simply takes on a more pluralistic character in everything it does—reveling in its diversity. Vital, growing congregations do not tend to focus their efforts on reaching one type of person. In fact, the pastors of most grow-ing congregations which do not have a diverse membership are embar-rassed by the fact, and see it as a definite flaw in their church.

Diversity in membership and forms of ministry and worship which speak to diverse groups makes a church more attractive to a larger share of the population. People feel welcome, regardless of their race, ethnicity, life-style, or social class. Further, this orientation allows a church to change in reaction to community change, and continue to grow.

Notes

1. Elmer L. Towns, John N. Vaughan, and David J Seifert, *The Complete Book of Church Growth* (Wheaton, Ill.: Tyndale House, 1981), 215.

2. Charles Chaney and Ron Lewis, *Design for Church Growth* (Nashville: Broadman Press, 1977).

3. Preliminary analysis from the Effective Christian Education Project: A Study of Protestant Congregations conducted by Search Institute.

4. Bill M. Sullivan, *Ten Steps to Breaking the 200 Barrier* (Kansas City: Beacon Hill Press of Kansas City, 1988), 25.

5. Wade Clark Roof, Dean R. Hoge, John E. Dyble, and C. Kirk Hadaway, "Factors Producing Growth or Decline in United Presbyterian Congregations" in *Understanding Church Growth and Decline: 1950-1978*, eds. Dean R. Hoge and David A. Roozen (New York: Pilgrim Press, 1979), 213.

6. Douglas Johnson, *Vitality Means Church Growth* (Nashville: Abingdon Press, 1989), 101-2.

7. Ibid., 99.

8. Lyle E. Schaller, *Assimilating New Members* (Nashville: Abingdon Press, 1978), 89.

11
The Community Context

Long before the term "church growth" was popularized by Donald McGavran and his disciples, the tendency for predominantly white, mainline churches located in prosperous, growing neighborhoods to grow faster than churches in deteriorating neighborhoods had been recognized by social scientists, historians, and church planners in the the United States. Not only were churches in blighted areas less likely to grow, they, in fact, often were experiencing rather severe *declines* in membership and attendance. It was a relationship which seemed obvious, undeniable, and even *deterministic* to the social observers early in this century.

According to H. Paul Douglass, who wrote this passage in 1935:

> Differences in human fortunes suffered by the church's immediate constituencies and changes in the fortunes due to changes in the environment largely control the institutional destinies of each particular church. Where the environment is prosperous and progressive the church can scarcely fail to "succeed." Where it is miserable and deteriorating the church can scarcely avoid failure.[1]

The deterministic view of church growth expressed by Douglass and others who described church trends in the late-nineteenth and early-twentieth centuries can be seen largely as a product of unusually rapid demographic changes affecting the cities during this period of American history. Between 1860 and 1890 Boston and New York City *more than tripled* in size and Philadelphia more than doubled. Rural to urban migration, coupled with waves of immigration from Europe, increased the pace of change in cities across America. New housing developments rapidly expanded the edge of the city into what was formerly rural territory. As these new neighborhoods were being settled, older neighborhoods closer to the downtown business district began to change in character, typically undergoing not one but a series of transitions—in terms of race, ethnicity, economic character, or land use. For the churches which were organized to serve urban neighborhoods, the swiftness of the change often was devastating. Churches grew rapidly as the population expanded, but they also began to decline rapidly when transition began. Many churches changed locations, some several times, in order to keep up with their members.[2]

The *pace* of urban growth and transition eventually slowed in most cities, but *the basic patterns persisted.* Throughout this century urban growth has been concentrated in the suburbs, while older neighborhoods typically have deteriorated and have seen various types of population transitions occur. Some urban neighborhoods have resisted decay, but they also have changed by becoming more heterogeneous in character—accommodating a much wider variety of persons in terms of age, life-style, socioeconomic status, and religion than was true when the neighborhoods were founded. In cities across America—where the bulk of the United States population resides—the only stable trend has been the certainty of neighborhood change.

These changes continue to affect local congregations. Research among the churches in many denominations—conservative, moderate, and liberal—has underscored the impact of the community context on church membership trends. For instance, in a study of membership growth and decline conducted among the churches of five predominantly white denominations in Memphis it was found that *all of the downtown churches were declining* during the late 1970s and early 1980s. Not one was growing or even plateaued. In older neighborhood locations the percentage of churches which were in decline moderated somewhat to 58 percent, whereas 12 percent of the churches were growing. In older suburbs the percentage declining was even lower, only 29 percent, and the percentage growing had increased to 40 percent. Newer suburbs were the areas most conducive to growth. Here, 72 percent of the churches were growing, while 20 percent were plateaued and only 8 percent were in decline.[3]

National studies of church growth among United Presbyterian and United Church of Christ congregations also underscored the impact of the community context on church growth and decline.[4] The influence was so strong and so pervasive that Dean Hoge and David Roozen concluded in *Understanding Church Growth and Decline,* "we believe that in mainline Protestant congregations, local contextual factors are relatively more powerful than local institutional factors."[5]

Even though there is near universal agreement among *social scientists* concerning the impact of the context or demographic setting on church growth, there is a definite tendency among writers in the church growth tradition, church consultants, and among denominational program personnel to either ignore or downplay the effect of the context. Lyle Schaller, for instance, often suggests that while the context impacts the church to some degree, it is of rather minor importance when compared to institutional factors. Most church-growth books ignore the subject altogether, although Peter Wagner acknowledges that racial transition can have a devastating effect on church growth. It can lead to the "disease" of "ethnikitis" which Wagner believes to be "the chief killer of churches in the U.S.A. today."[6]

The tendency to ignore or deny the impact of the context on church growth seems odd because most *pastors* of predominantly white churches are well aware that it is much easier to grow a church in the suburbs than it is in any other urban location. So why the neglect? One explanation may be that since the context rarely can be changed by the church, those who are in the business of helping churches achieve growth do not wish to deal with a force which is beyond the ability of the church to control. They have focused instead on areas which *can* be addressed by actions of the congregation.

It would seem somewhat shortsighted, however, to ignore a major source of growth and decline. Proper planning can only proceed on the basis of factual knowledge. And if a declining or plateaued church wishes to grow it must understand why it is *not growing*. The reasons may have little to do with the context in some cases, but if the lack of growth *is* related to the context, then the proper steps to achieve growth must be informed by the constraints imposed by the context. A predominantly white church which remains in a black neighborhood must do more than start a visitation program or hire a great "pulpiteer." A rural church which finds itself surrounded by affluent housing developments must do more than hold a revival or pave its parking lot. And a suburban church, grown accustomed to easy growth, must do something *other* than blame its pastor and call another when population growth in the area finally comes to an end and the church settles onto a plateau.

The character of the social context makes it *that much easier or that much harder for a church to grow.* The impact will rarely *determine* whether a church will grow or decline, but it will tend to either constrain growth or make growth more likely. The effect is there and it should be understood if a church expects either to *overcome* the impact of its environment or to *exploit* that environment.

The Nature of the Relationship

The relationship between the context and church growth is implicit in many areas of church and denominational planning. For instance, most denominations have concentrated their efforts to start new (non-ethnic) churches in growing suburban and exurban areas. The reason for this is simple. Most people are unwilling to drive long distances to attend church, so when new suburban developments are constructed it makes sense for a denomination to start new congregations there areas. If they do not, at least some of their members who live in these are likely to drop out or to begin attending nearby churches affiliated with other denominations.

New suburban churches have an advantage over most other congregations in at least two respects. First, they are located in areas where population growth is occurring, and second, their newness allows these congregations to assimilate new members more easily than is possible in the typical older congregation. When taken together, these factors allow most new suburban churches to grow.

By planting new churches in the suburbs denominations implicitly (and in some cases explicitly) recognize the impact of the context on church growth. In this case, new churches are attempting to exploit the environment rather than to overcome it.

The Impact of Population Growth

Previous church growth research has demonstrated a strong relationship between population growth in the community surrounding a church and the growth of the congregation. It is a relationship which varies from city to city, however, according to the rapidity of change and the extent to which churches are concentrated in areas which are experiencing the most dramatic population gains or losses. But it also is a relationship which exists to some extent in *all communities*. Population increase encourages church growth, whereas population loss is associated with membership stagnation or decline.

In order to examine the nature of this relationship more fully, all Southern Baptist churches were asked in the 1983 Uniform Church Letter if the area within one-mile radius of their location was growing, stable, or declining in population. As can be seen in figure 11.1, a full 66 percent of metropolitan congregations which had significant membership growth from 1983 to 1987 indicated *in 1983* that the surrounding area was growing in population. By contrast, only 34 percent of plateaued churches and 24 percent of declining congregations were in areas experiencing population growth. Only a small proportion of Southern Baptist churches said that their community was declining in population in 1983. However, those which did so were much more likely to experience membership decline in the years following 1983.

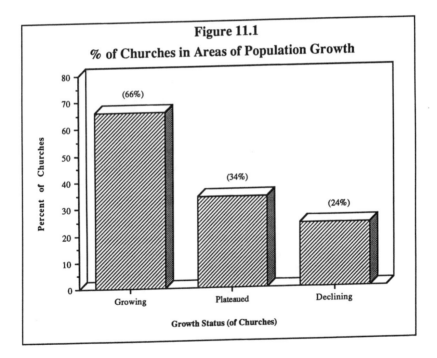

Figure 11.1
% of Churches in Areas of Population Growth

Another effort to explore the relationship between church growth and population growth was made by examining the characteristics of the zip code area in which a church was located. Population data are available for all United States zip codes from the U. S. Census Bureau for 1970 and 1980, and 1989 estimates can be obtained from private demographic data vendors. A zip code data file was obtained from one of these data vendors which contained both census data and 1989 population estimates. This file was then matched with a set of metropolitan Southern Baptist churches which had returned a lengthy church-growth questionnaire.

Percent change in the population within a zip code produced a strong correlation with church growth. Growing churches are much more likely to be located in areas experiencing higher levels of population growth during the years 1980 to 1989 (48 percent of growing churches were in areas of growing population). By contrast, only 12 percent of plateaued churches and 20 percent of declining churches were located in zip codes which experienced higher levels of population growth.

It is clear from these data that population growth tends to encourage church growth. Not *all* churches in growing areas experience membership growth, but a large proportion will do so. Conversely, population stagnation does not ensure a membership plateau or decline, but it makes it all the more likely. An increasing supply of residents means more potential visitors who lack a current church affiliation and who are in search of a new "church home." Such areas make membership growth easier than do communities where there are few newcomers and where existing residents have already made their decision to opt into our out of the church.

New Housing

All types of population growth are not equally beneficial to the typical conservative or mainline church. Population growth may come in the form of another race, another income group, apartment dwellers, or some other population which the typical Anglo-Protestant church has difficulty attracting. For this reason, several other census questions were more strongly related to church growth than was the sheer increase in numbers of persons. One of these questions dealt with new housing.

The proportion of housing in a community which is newly constructed taps population growth, but it also gets at another contextual dimension which is related to church growth. Areas which are growing *through the construction of new housing* tend to be suburban or exurban (spotty areas of new-housing development surrounding the urban sprawl) in character—rather than inner-city areas where larger ethnic families are beginning to displace small "empty- nester" families. Population growth is occurring in these latter areas, but it is growth which typically does not help most traditional Anglo churches to grow.

Figure 11.2 shows that 60 percent of growing churches are located in zip codes where there is a high proportion of new housing, as compared to only 24 percent of plateaued churches and 27 percent of declining churches. Plateaued and declining churches tend to be located in areas with older housing stock. Additional census data reveals that almost half (48 percent) of plateaued and declining churches are in areas where a large proportion of the housing was constructed in 1959 or earlier, as compared to only 21 percent of growing churches.

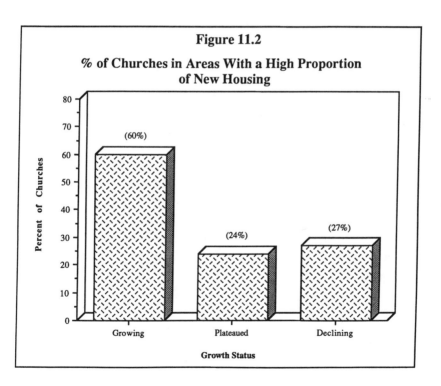

Figure 11.2

% of Churches in Areas With a High Proportion of New Housing

Racial Composition and Change

Since the vast majority of Southern Baptist churches are predominantly white, it came as no surprise that the proportion of blacks in the zip code was strongly related to church membership change. Of the *declining* churches which returned the church growth questionnaire, 31 percent were located in zip codes where there was a high proportion of blacks. By contrast, 14 percent of plateaued churches and only 7 percent of growing churches were located in such areas.

Zip code data also indicates a substantial correlation between *racial transition* and membership decline. Churches in areas where the proportion of blacks in the community was increasing were more likely to be on the plateau or in decline than were churches in areas where racial transition was not occurring.

These relationships speak strongly to the racism that continues in American society. In Los Angeles, for instance, many communities are stable mixtures of Anglos and Hispanics or Asians and Anglos, but residential segregation for African-Americans is as strong in Los Angeles as it is in Birmingham, Alabama. Areas are either under 20 percent black or they are over 80 percent black. "White flight" still occurs in American cities, although not at the pace that once was true. It hurts white churches because their members are a part of the flight and because predominantly white churches have a difficult time attracting or accepting African-Americans into their fellowship.

Some would say that a racially integrated church is impossible to sustain and that a church cannot change as the community changes if that change involves racial transition. These are self-fulfilling prophecies, however, which are contradicted by the existence of a relatively small number of racially integrated churches and a large number of churches which have successfully changed from predominantly white to predominantly black as the community experienced a similar transition.

Age Structure

In a previous chapter it was noted that churches which have a high proportion of members in the baby boom generation were much more likely to grow than were churches which were less effective in reaching this large component of the population. For this reason it might be anticipated that the best areas for church growth would be those zip codes with the largest proportions of baby boomers. Such was not the case, however. The best areas for growth were those zip codes with a larger proportion of persons in the 45 to 54 age group in 1989 (those born 1935 to 1944)—in other words, the generation which preceded the baby boomers.

Perhaps this finding should not seem so odd. After all, baby boomers are less likely to attend church than are the generations which preceded them. Further, baby boomers are at this point much less likely to be *home owners* than are those born between 1935 and 1944. A large proportion of baby boomers still reside in apartments and one of the major failings of Protestant churches in America has been the relative inability to reach persons who live in multifamily housing. Our churches are effective in reaching the traditional home-owning family with children—a group which has become increasingly rare in American society (only 27 percent of U. S. households were married couples with children in 1988 and the proportion which also are homeowners lowers this figure to only 20 percent of all households).[7]

So even though the churches which are reaching baby boomers are more likely to grow, this population is somewhat harder to reach than is the generation born between 1935 and 1944. Zip codes with large numbers of baby boomers are also quite favorable to church growth, but not to the extent of zip codes with large proportion of residents born between 1935 and 1944.

As might be expected, the poorest areas for growth were those zip codes with a large proportion of persons in the older-age categories. In fact, churches in areas with a high proportion of persons ages 65 and over were more likely *to decline* or be on the plateau than were churches in areas which had a low proportion of residents in this age group. This finding has nothing to do with these people being old, however, because it is well known that older Americans have higher average levels of church attendance than any other age group. The negative relationship between the proportion of elderly persons and church growth exists because areas dominated by the elderly are more likely to be declining or stable in population.

Socioeconomic Status

Many economic and social status measures were also related to church growth. Zip codes with high levels of poverty, low education, high unemployment, and low-income levels tended to have churches which were plateaued or declining. Conversely, areas where the socioeconomic picture was brighter were more likely to be home to growing Southern Baptist congregations.

These findings speak again to the relative inability of most churches to accept persons who are different from the homogeneous groups which makes up the bulk of their membership.

Some Odd Findings Regarding Declining Churches

One of the most peculiar features of the relationship between the context and church growth is the fact that *plateaued* churches and *declining* churches seem to differ relatively little in the character of their locations. In fact, in some ways the declining churches seem to be in better demographic locations for growth on average than are plateaued churches. Apparently this results from the tendency of plateaued churches to be located in areas where the demographic context is neither particularly good, nor particularly bad. Declining churches, on the other hand, tend to be located in areas that are either *very bad* or not bad at all. For instance, there is a much larger proportion of declining churches in zip codes with high unemployment and at the same time a slightly higher proportion in zip codes with very low unemployment—as compared to the proportion of plateaued churches in these same areas. Similar results were seen for the proportion of the population living in poverty, median income, median-housing value, median rent, percentage of persons age seventy-five to eighty-four, and percent black.

This may seem a little confusing, but it is interpretable. Decline tends to result from either a very poor demographic setting or from internal (institutional) problems which can occur *in any location—even in areas which would seem very conducive to growth.* A plateau, on the other hand, is somewhat less likely in very good locations or in very poor locations. Plateaued churches typically are in a maintenance mode, doing an adequate job in most areas, while avoiding severe internal conflict. In very good areas, churches in this type of maintenance mode tend to grow in spite of themselves, whereas in very poor areas, they find themselves declining. Thus, plateaued churches are more often found in rural areas, small towns, and in stable urban neighborhoods than in growing suburbs or in areas undergoing severe population loss or racial transition.

Another confounding influence with regard to declining churches is their greater tendency to be what Schaller calls "ex-neighborhood" congregations.[8] That is, most of their members once lived in the area nearby the church but have since moved away and must drive back in order to worship. For these churches, the quality of the surrounding zip code is irrelevant. Whether the area is improving in its demographic character, as many are, or whether the area is deteriorating, the church will still decline. Why? The answer is simple. The church is no longer a community institution. Local residents will not know anyone in the church, nor are they likely to meet anyone from the church in the community, and consequently they will not be *invited* to attend. This means, of course, that the church is dependent for visitors on "walk-ins" from the local community, and these individuals will quickly see that the church contains few persons like themselves. Unless the church is unusually friendly to outsiders, which most ex-neighborhood churches are not, the visitors will decide that this congregation is not for them.

Visitation and other church-growth emphases also will be difficult for the ex-neighborhood church, because community residents will be confronted by persons who live miles away. In the real world, of course, ex-neighborhood churches are extremely unlikely to conduct any sort of outreach effort in the community surrounding the church building. Their members left the area for a reason, they return to worship because it is *their church*, but they will not reach out to others in the community unless the church is threatened with closing. By the time it reaches this stage, however, it will be too late for the church to begin to "re-reach" its community unless the association or local judicatory is able essentially to start a *new* congregation in the facility. This is done by organizing a core group of community residents who will come into the ex-neighborhood church *en masse* and slowly take over leadership and financial responsibility from the older, dying congregation.

How Churches Adjust to Neighborhood Change

Churches typically are structured as if they served stable, cohesive parishes where little competition existed for members, rather than the mobile, noncohesive, heterogeneous communities in which they actually find themselves. Their membership is drawn primarily from neighborhoods within several miles of the church building and church leaders consider this area their territory, or parish. It is an approach which seems well designed for village life, but certainly not for mobile urban America, where over three quarters of the United States population now resides.

When a church is new, however, the traditional Protestant congregation seems well suited to its environment and survives quite well in what I have called the "competitive parish"—a setting where churches of various denominations share a given geographic area (parish) and compete for members. When most churches are organized in these parishes they begin with a key group of leaders and workers who form the core of the church. This initial group of members sets the style and identity of the congregation—things which tend to remain quite stable over time. Informal rules of dress and behavior emerge and close-knit friendship groups form within the congregation. The church is a social institution, and like all social institutions, it will find change progressively more difficult as it ages.

The initial members of a new church are drawn from nearby neighborhoods, and so the church naturally takes on the class and life-style character of the surrounding local community. Also, since most new neighborhoods begin with families in the same stage of the life cycle and the same racial character, the neighborhood is initially quite homogeneous and often has a strong community spirit and self-conscious identity. Churches in this situation tend to grow until the wave of new-housing construction passes them by.

When local churches cannot depend upon a steady supply of new residents with similar social characteristics, they begin to experience growth problems which reflect the inevitability of neighborhood change and a certain weakness in the structure of the typical Protestant church. Soon after they are built, urban neighborhoods begin to change, often quickly, sometimes slowly; but change they do until the structure of the local community becomes radically different from what it was when the neighborhood first developed. The process continues as old residents move and are replaced by newcomers with different social characteristics, and as residents age and their children move away. The once homogeneous community becomes steadily more heterogeneous, or it may change in character completely, becoming black rather than white, or Hispanic rather than Anglo.

These changes bring problems for most churches because once a congregation completes its mission to reach its community and to become a stable, viable institution, it tends to change its focus from mission to maintenance. In other words, it alters its definition of its community from those who live in the neighborhoods surrounding the church to those persons who are actually participating in the life of the congregation. It becomes client-centered rather than outreach-oriented. In this mode the church develops and maintains a set of programs which are designed to meet the needs of its members. As long as the needs of the current church members are similar to those who live in the local community, there is no problem. But this is rarely the case—at least for very long.

As the community changes, the needs of the residents also change and if the church is seen as unresponsive to these needs, new residents will not be attracted to the church. The congregation will continue to attract a dwindling supply of newcomers who "fit" the style of the current congregation and who are attracted to its programs, while the bulk of newcomers will remain outside the church or look for another congregation which is more responsive to their needs. The net result of this process, which may occur very slowly and almost imperceptibly to the congregation, is that the church and its community begin to diverge in character. The church remains largely the same in terms of its basic composition, while the surrounding neighborhoods steadily change. Over time, a gap develops between the church and its geographic community. Whereas the church once largely reflected the age structure, class character, and ethnicity of the local community, now there are major differences. And the differences tend to increase. The church remains solidly middle class and white, while the community becomes poorer or of mixed ethnic character; the church building is kept in good repair, but nearby housing becomes somewhat "seedy." The membership increases in age while the community attracts younger residents.

Apartment complexes are built on vacant land or displace existing single-family housing, yet the church is only able to reach traditional home-owning families.

In most cases, members still are drawn from surrounding neighborhoods, although as members move the church may develop more of a regional flavor than it had initially. In the worst cases, however, nearly everyone moves away, and they only return to their old "parish" for worship services—except for a few elderly members who have not had the option or inclination to move. What was once a community church has become an "ex-neighborhood church." This is a pattern which affects many churches in older urban neighborhoods, and is particularly likely when racial transition occurs.

It should be apparent from this discussion that most congregations do not consciously adjust to changes in their demographic settings. They remain largely the same in terms of composition, style, and program, and members hope that enough people will find their church as warm and inviting as they do. The traditional family-oriented church with an adequate program tends to experience membership growth when the church is young and when it is in the midst of homogeneous growing neighborhoods, but it tends to plateau and eventually decline when population growth ends and as the church and its community eventually diverge in character. It is a process which helps give many churches the appearance of an inevitable "life cycle" from birth, to youth, to maturity, and finally to death.

To be sure, some churches do adjust to their changing surroundings, but usually only in response to crisis, and often the response cannot be described as being in the best interest of the local community. Threatened by membership decline, racial transition, or simply attracted by the growth potential of the suburbs, churches all across America have moved in order to flee a "bad setting" for a "good setting." Rather than responding to the changes in their community and changing along with the community, they have redefined their community as their members and have chosen to follow them into new areas. In some cities, this has meant not one move but two, three, or even four. Little thought is given to the local residents in this process because the church is not seen as *their* church. The church belongs to the current members, and it is theirs to dispose of as they see fit.

In some cases churches which relocate have been able to sell their existing building to other congregations which are indigenous to the local community. And in other situations the church can work with the association or local judicatory to begin a new church in the old facility. However, all too often, the land is sold to the highest bidder and the community loses a church.

The strong relationship between demographic change and church membership change exists largely because churches fail to adjust to changes in the community context. If churches were able to become more heterogeneous along with the local community; if churches were able to reach apartment dwellers as well as home owners; if churches were able to accept singles and divorced persons as well as married couples with children; and if churches were able to make the transition from white to black or Anglo to Hispanic as transition occurred, then there would not be a strong relationship between most measures of the community context and church growth. But because most churches have not been able to do these things, the relationship remains quite strong.

It should be added that the above findings and generalizations are true for predominantly white, Anglo congregations. No research has been conducted as yet on the impact of the context on ethnic or African-American churches. We would expect, however, that a relationship would exist between the growth of ethnic churches and demographic change, but that the direction of many of the relationships would be different than for Anglo churches. Obviously, an increase in the black population would be expected to help, not hurt, the growth of African-American churches.

What This Means for Church Planning

The first step for a church planning committee which is concerned about the direction of their church is to understand and accept the dynamics which are operative in the church and its community. The second step is for the church to decide that it must change if it wishes to grow. It also is hoped that church leaders will decide that they should change by more effectively ministering to their community—rather than by moving to a "better" location. Many church members will be unaware that their church is subtly excluding others who are "not like us" and will not understand why anyone would not enjoy their church. But once church leaders recognize that their congregation is diverging from the local community and that it is becoming less able to reach and minister to new residents, and once they decide that this is something to which the church must respond (other than by moving), it becomes possible for strategic planning to alter the course of the congregation.

Clearly, one of the major components of strategic planning is the evaluation of the "environment." And in this case the environment includes the surrounding demographic setting as well as *the church itself*. In this phase of analysis the church can estimate the extent to which it has diverged from the local community; it can determine the needs which exist among local residents; and it can evaluate the extent to which the church unconsciously has become a client-centered organization.

Through the planning process a church will develop a new role to replace the worn-out sense of purpose which guided the congregation through its formative years. This new purpose will include, it is hoped, a renewed emphasis on reaching its geographic community.

Although all churches must design their own strategies for becoming responsive to their communities, there are certain things which are essential for nearly any church which finds itself in a community which has become more heterogeneous in terms of age, ethnicity, life-style, and income. Such churches should take the following actions.

(1) Adjust the style of worship and Sunday School to fit the broadest segment of the community, rather than just to fit current members.

(2) Incorporate elements into the worship service which respond directly to the interests and needs of all major segments of the community (by asking them what they would like in a church). This may include adding elements of traditional black worship to traditional white worship, solos in languages other than English, a sermon preached bilingually, and contemporary Christian music (along with its rock beat) for baby boomers who were raised on rock and roll, or even backwoods, country hymns if new residents are rural migrants.

(3) Provide separate Sunday School classes, home Bible studies or cell groups, worship services, and other such units for any homogeneous group that does not feel comfortable attending joint meetings or which desires a homogeneous small-group setting along with joint, multicultural worship.

(4) Create visible symbols for the community that the church is open to local residents, that it wants them to attend as they are, and that it is

concerned about their needs. Such symbols may come in the form of ministries without ulterior motives, cross-cultural events at the church, neighborhood renovation projects, an associate minister who represents a large minority group in the community, and so forth.

In short the church must make a conscious effort to embrace diversity, so that it can accept newcomers of all kinds. Anything which broadcasts openness, concern for all, and the willingness to accept new people who are different and to provide a place for them where they can feel accepted will help in this process. Such a church may not grow as fast as a church in the rapidly expanding suburbs, but unlike thousands of traditional homogeneous, Anglo-Protestant churches in older neighborhoods across America, such churches are likely to *grow* rather than to plateau or decline. They also will be less affected by further changes in their demographic settings. They will change along with the community rather than maintaining themselves as vestigial remains of a community which has long been dead.

A final word regarding planning and dealing with the context is that the process should not end. Churches should institute a process of periodic reevaluation so that they can avoid diverging from their communities in the future and thereby ensure that their goals are meeting the needs of their members, of community residents, and of the most recent newcomers to the community. Such churches will never find that their membership trends are *determined* by the environment.

Notes

1. H. Paul Douglas, *The Protestant Church as a Social Institution* (New York: Russell and Russell, 1935), 237-38.

2. Sydney E. Ahlstrom, *A Religious History of the American People*, (Garden City, N.J.: Doubleday, 1975), 2:193-94.

3. C. Kirk Hadaway, "Church Growth (and Decline) in a Southern City," *Review of Religious Research* 23 (1982): 372-86.

4. Wade Clark Roof, Dean R. Hoge, John E. Dyble and C. Kirk Hadaway, "Factors Producing Growth or Decline in United Presbyterian Congregations" in *Understanding Church Growth and Decline*, eds. Dean R. Hoge and David A. Roozen (New York: Pilgrim Press, 1979), 198-223; William J. McKinney, Jr., "Performance of United Church of Christ Congregations in Massachusetts and in Pennsylvania" in *Understanding Church Growth and Decline*, eds. Dean R. Hoge and David A. Roozen (New York: Pilgrim Press, 1979), 224-47.

5. Dean R. Hoge and David A. Roozen, "Some Sociological Conclusions About Church Trends" in *Understanding Church Growth and Decline*, 326.

6. C. Peter Wagner, *Your Church Can Grow*, rev. ed. (Ventura, Calif.: Regal Books, 1984), 146.

7. *Research Alert* 7:14 (1989): 2.

8. Lyle E. Schaller, *Hey, That's Our Church* (Nashville: Abingdon Press, 1975), 51.

12
The Primary Principles

Many things are related to church growth. That much should be clear from the previous chapters. Growing churches are different from plateaued and declining congregations, and these differences can be seen in how growing churches do things, in their social characteristics, in their locations, in their priorities, and in their "spirit." A growing church feels different. It feels alive because it is alive.

Not all of the factors which contribute to church growth are equal in strength. The differences among growing, plateaued, and declining churches on a number of survey questions were immense, while in other cases there was only a slight tendency for growing congregations to score somewhat higher or somewhat lower than did plateaued or declining churches. For instance, several measures of evangelism showed huge differences between growing and nongrowing churches in activity and emphasis. On the other hand, the relationships between most measures of pastoral performance and church growth were quite small.

This chapter seeks was to determine which grow-related influences or principles were most *critical* for church growth. This is not simply a matter of strength, it is a matter of impact—measured while holding other church growth influences constant. The results show that some things which have long been thought to be critical are, in fact, critical. Other factors are not critical to church growth, but they are helpful, while still others are best regarded as playing a supportive role—forming a stable base from which the critical factors can work.

What Is Critical?

Evangelistic Outreach

The most important thing a church can do if it wishes to grow is evangelistic outreach and recruitment. An evangelism/outreach scale which combined fourteen questions dealing with evangelistic activity, recruitment, evangelism campaigns, visitation, mass mailouts to community residents, evangelism training, and other actions produced a huge relationship with church growth. As was noted in chapter 1, and as can be seen in figure 1.2, 42 percent of growing churches scored high on the evangelism/outreach scale, as compared to only 11 percent of plateaued churches and 6 percent of declining churches.

The strong relationship between evangelism and church growth was subjected to an exhaustive series of tests to determine whether there was something about the pastor, the community, the structure of the church, or a host of other things which could account for at least part of this relationship. In statistical terms, many controls were put into effect to see if the impact of evangelism was independent of other factors.

In all tests that were made, the evangelism/outreach scale remained the strongest predicter of church growth. Not only that, the magnitude of the relationship was only slightly diminished when powerful statistical controls were put into effect for such things as the demographic environment and the age structure of the congregation.

Evangelistic outreach and general recruitment efforts help churches in all community settings—except, perhaps, in those situations where all of the church members live miles away from the church and have little in common with local residents. In less extreme situations, however, recruitment efforts may help a church in a declining neighborhood to "hold its own" and avoid membership losses. Similarly, evangelistic activity may help a church in a stable neighborhood achieve growth and actually lower the proportion of unchurched residents in its community. For churches in growing neighborhoods, evangelistic outreach and recruitment efforts may allow growth to be especially dramatic. In addition, the efforts allow such churches to establish evangelism as the normal state of affairs among their members—so that when population growth in the area ends, the church will be able to do evangelistic outreach when it becomes *necessary* for growth.

The evangelistic orientation of a congregation does not only refer to programmed forms of evangelistic outreach, such as Sunday School visitation or witnessing "SWAT teams." The evangelistic church may include such things (and most do), but the key element is not a program. Instead, it is an open orientation to the outside world which says "we are interested in your needs, we want for you to know Christ as we have come to know Him, and we would like for you to join with us in our struggle to learn, grow, and serve." Evangelistic churches create a sense that witnessing about one's faith is normal and that it can occur anywhere, that the church has something to offer and members want to tell others about it, and that evangelism means more than presenting a tract to someone.

The outreach-oriented church is open and accepting of newcomers. If it were not, why would the effort be made to draw in others? The outreach-oriented church does not use a single method of evangelism. If only one method was used, only a small number of members could be involved. Evangelistic outreach and recruitment are the primary methods through which plateaued churches achieve breakout growth and are the primary ways that growing churches *continue to grow.*

Age Structure

Another feature which has an impact on growth—an impact almost as great as that of evangelism—is the age structure of the congregation. Growing churches have a healthy mix of ages among their memberships and tend to incorporate a large proportion of baby boomer families and young single adults. Growing churches do not tend to be dominated by the elderly—except perhaps in Sun City, Arizona; Tampa, Florida; and other communities with a heavy concentration of retirees.

In one sense, "maintaining a healthy age structure" can be seen more as a characteristic of a healthy congregation than as a growth principle. It may seem ludicrous to tell a church, "develop a healthy age structure and you will grow." And, in fact, that advice would not be a very helpful thing to tell a church planning committee or a pastor. On the other hand, it is important to tell such a committee or pastor to pay attention to their age structure and to recognize when it begins to diverge from the age structure of the surrounding community.

Baby boomers (both single and married) and the children of baby boomers constitute a very large proportion of the American population.

Is it any wonder that churches which have been able to reach this group are growing? Simply having a fairly large number of these individuals in one's church makes the congregation more attractive to other baby boomers. The church also is likely to have an active singles ministry and to take programming for children seriously—out of necessity.

Churches which are dominated by older adults are much less likely to grow than are churches dominated by baby boomers (or churches which are not dominated by any one age group). Of course this will change as the baby boomers turn into older adults. In about eighteen years church-growth theorists will begin to tout seniors ministry as the new key to church growth. There even may be a new surge in bus ministries as churches which want to grow are compelled to provide transportation for aging baby boomers. Even today, churches could do a lot more to reach older residents in their communities. These persons have needs, at least some are unchurched; all could benefit from a church relationship; and the church could benefit from them as well. Older persons tend to have higher levels of faith maturity, and they have more discretionary time. For these reasons, members who are retirement age often make some of the best Sunday School teachers and outreach leaders.

For most churches which are currently *dominated* by older adults, however, the future is not bright, and it is no surprise that few are growing. Some of these congregations are "ex-neighborhood churches" and others are located in communities in the midst of population decline. Once a church reaches the point where it is dominated by older adults, it has long since lost the ability to attract younger persons. There will be no programs for younger adults, and there will be few, if any, resources for children. There is likely to be no youth program, much less a ministry for young singles. In short, churches dominated by the elderly will be less likely to meet the needs of potential members who are younger than the current membership.

Churches which are dominated by older adults also are likely to have many long-term members. The issue here is not the age of members, it is the tendency of long-term members of any age to be less open to changes in the structure of the church and to be less accepting of newcomers.

It is not that churches which have many older adults cannot grow, or that unchurched senior adults cannot be a source of church growth for a congregation which is interested in reaching out to elderly persons in the community—as opposed to caring for older adults who have been with the congregation for many years. It is just that the typical church which is *dominated* by senior adults has many characteristics which preclude growth.

Commitment and Interest

A *third* factor which appears to be essential to church growth is a high level of commitment to and interest in the church, which is expressed by a large proportion of the membership attending each Sunday.

Like the age structure of a church, the commitment/interest level of a congregation cannot easily be altered by the actions of the pastor and church leaders. Efforts to raise the commitment level of members are usually directed at the consciences of members who are sitting in the worship services (persons who are fairly committed, or they wouldn't be there). These efforts rarely work. Members are stung by the pastor for their lack of commitment and involvement in the life of the church. "We need Sunday School teachers, but few volunteer." "We need people to visit prospects, but few show up for Monday night visitation." "When it rains, when a relative comes into town, or when the weather is perfect for golf or a day at the park, the church loses out in the balancing of priorities." All this ends with a line something like, "where is your commitment to God and to this church?"

The fact of the matter is, guilt is a very poor long-term motivator. It may help bring church members to a concert by the children's choir or to help with a community census, but it will not keep large numbers of members coming back for visitation, nor will it affect the proportion of the congregation that actually attends worship on an average Sunday. But even if guilt *could* affect attendance, the persons who need to hear the message in order to have their guilt level raised are not likely to do so. They are asleep, at the park, having brunch, mowing the lawn, out of town for the weekend, or just relaxing.

To raise the proportion of members who attend on an average Sunday, a church must have something good and meaningful to offer so that members will want to be there whenever they can. Do most members leave your church after worship saying, "that was wonderful"? If they do, then your church probably has a high proportion of its members who attend each week.

Of course, why members are likely to say "that was wonderful" will vary widely from congregation to congregation. In some churches it may be the pastor's sermon which is the primary "draw"—though this is very rare. Still, many of the largest churches in America depend very heavily on their pastors for growth and for the involvement of members. In most other growing churches the reasons for satisfaction, interest, and excitement about the church are more complex. Typically, it is a combination of great meaning and great spirit. Some churches have more of one than they do of the other. A few churches seem to embody both in equal measure and at very high levels. These churches are growing rapidly and have a high level of commitment and involvement on the part of their members.

It also should be added that it generally takes more than a "wonderful" worship service to create the kind of commitment that keeps people coming back week after week. Warm fellowship, concern for one another, opportunities for meaningful service, and a seriousness about learning all contribute to the sense that the church is a good place to be. Duty will provide some level of motivation for many members, but for most churches to grow, a sense of duty is not enough. Something tangible must be there which members not only receive, but that they create themselves.

What About the Pastor?

Pastor search committees generally look for either the best preacher they can find or for the best "shepherd" they can hire, depending on the needs of the congregation for either a "good show" on Sunday or for nurturing. Large churches and churches interested in growth lean toward the pastor as preacher. Older, plateaued congregations tend to lean toward the pastor as nurturer—someone who is friendly, caring, outgoing, likable, and always has time for people. There are other pastoral models, of course, but these two are most common. Unfortunately, looking for either type of a pastor is misguided, at least if a church has any interest in growth.

Preaching ability is virtually unrelated to growth, and the pastor who is primarily a caretaker-nurturer is unlikely to emphasize the things which a congregation must do in order to grow. It should be mentioned, however, that if a church is able to attract a "preaching machine," it probably will see some growth. And if a church has built itself on a previous "preaching machine," it will likely decline unless it calls another. However, as all pastor search committees should realize, the supply of great orators is limited, and they are unlikely to find one unless they are very large or very lucky. If they are very lucky and find a young future preaching star, they also should be aware that this future star is unlikely to stay with them long and that they may not be able to find another.

Most objective measures of pastoral performance and competency are unrelated to church growth. That is a fact. It is also true, however, that when churches begin to grow rapidly after years on the plateau it usually has something to do with a new (or renewed) pastor.

So what kind of a pastor should a church call if it is interested in growth? The answer is a pastor who fits the model of a catalytic leader. More specifically, a church should look for someone with vision, and who understands how to work with and lead people in a loving and encouraging way. This sort of pastor is interested in developing people and in allowing them and empowering them to use their gifts. The catalytic pastor cares about people and is available to offer counsel, but does not allow his or her church to drift aimlessly. And finally, the catalytic pastor should have a great interest in evangelism if the church is going to see growth, since it is possible for a catalytic leader to lead a church to achieve goals other than growth. Additional characteristics of the catalytic leader can be found in Bob Dale's book, *Pastoral Leadership*.

What Is Helpful?

There are things which have a substantial effect on growth, but which are not *essential* to growth. They help churches grow, but it is possible to grow without them. The first of these deals with how visitors are treated. Churches where something special is happening and where members are telling others about their wonderful church will have visitors. Some of these visitors will join. It helps, however, if visitors are treated as if they are welcome and valued. Part of this is friendliness. Another part is symbolic. Growing churches are more likely to provide special parking and seating for visitors. Visitors are recognized in worship services in ways that make them feel wanted, but not embarrassed.

In a recent visit to a church in Nashville, I drove to the parking lot behind the church and was confronted by three doors, none of which had a sign telling where they led. No one was in the parking lot to welcome visitors or to help them find the proper Sunday School class or the sanctuary. There also was no special parking for visitors. Once inside the church (I picked the right door) there was a sign for the preschool department, but no one to tell me which rooms were the right ones for my children. When the proper classrooms were identified by asking another parent, I tried to find the sanctuary. My first attempt led to a blind alley. I tried another floor and had to ask directions. No one offered to help, even though I appeared to be lost. Visitors were welcomed in the worship service, but there was no effort to have members give me a personal greeting. I was asked to fill out a visitor's card, but there was no card in the pew rack, nor in any pew around me. Even though less than 150 people were in the worship service, I left with only one person having recognized that I was a visitor, and thanking me for attending. This is not how a church should treat visitors. This church did not expect visitors, and members apparently didn't really care whether or not I was there.

A second thing which helps churches to grow is the use of the Sunday School Growth Spiral or some other special programs that puts in place organizational procedures which encourage church growth. Participation in such a plan implies intentionality on the part of the church. It says that the church is acting on its identity as an evangelical congregation and is trying to reach people for Christ. Involvement allows a church to assimilate those who are attracted through outreach efforts.

A third thing which helps churches grow is proper staffing for growth. An adequate staff is not essential for a church to grow off the plateau, but there is a limit to the amount of growth a church can sustain without adding staff. The more members a church has, the heavier is the work load on the pastor. Churches that want to keep growing will add staff in accordance with accepted denominational guidelines. Failure to do this may eventually lead to a plateau or to pastor burnout. Both can be avoided if a church recognizes that proper staffing is not a luxury but a proven way to see that growth continues.

What Is Supportive?

Many other factors can best be seen as supportive of growth—as things that go along with the primary principles. They are things which should not be ignored. They add to growth by providing a firm foundation through which the primary principles can operate. The first of these is Sunday School, in its role of teaching, fellowship, and assimilation. The role of Sunday School as outreach has been included as part of the most important "primary principle"—that of outreach and evangelism. An overall rating of Sunday School, which was developed by combining questions dealing with Sunday School for adults, youth, and children, produced a very strong correlation with church growth. Growing churches tend to have strong, effective Sunday School programs for all age groups. The independent effect of Sunday School was relatively weak, however. This suggests that a strong Sunday School may be a necessary but is not a sufficient condition for growth. Many nongrowing churches have what they consider to be strong Sunday Schools. However, if they do not use the Sunday School for outreach, if they neglect other forms of evangelistic outreach, if they are not reaching out to their immediate community, and if their members are not committed to and excited about the church to any great degree, then growth is unlikely.

It could be argued that one cannot have a strong Sunday School without evangelism, since outreach is an integral part of the Sunday School design. This may be true, but many churches have what they consider to be a strong, highly organized Sunday School, but give only lip service to outreach. They do Sunday School for its teaching function rather than for its outreach function.

Quality worship also is a necessary, but not sufficient, condition for growth. Take it away and growth potential will decrease. Evangelistic churches, with highly committed members, which are reaching their communities for Christ, tend to have exciting worship services.

Following Sunday School and worship as critical supportive factors to church growth are, in order of importance, planning and goal setting, lay leadership (and the willingness to change), new member assimilation, and an emphasis on prayer and spirituality.

What Also Must Be Considered?

All churches are not created equal. They exist in different settings, and they are different ages. These things cannot be changed. They can be overcome or even exploited, of course, and some would argue that because they can be overcome they are irrelevant. But this is not the case. Whether a church is overcoming its setting or not, that setting has an effect on the church. It cannot be avoided. From a growth perspective, the setting (as well as the age of a church) makes it that much easier or that much harder for a church to grow.

The overall impact and independent effect of the demographic setting is almost as strong as that of evangelism/outreach and the age structure of the congregation on church growth. Unlike institutional correlates of growth like Sunday School, worship, and various forms of ministry, the effect of the demographic setting acts independently of other church-growth influences. Churches with one feature of institutional quality tend to have other features of institutional quality, but the demographic setting is virtually unrelated to any measure of quality or vitality. For this reason, even when statistical controls are put into effect, the impact of the context or setting remains strong.

The most powerful and independent contextual correlates of growth include the proportion of housing constructed since 1975, racial transition, and the purchasing power of community residents. Areas that are growing in population and that are growing in population through the construction of new housing are most likely to be home to growing churches. These areas tend to be new suburban and exurban areas where new residents are likely to be home-owning young couples with children and home-owning adults who are slightly older than the baby boomers (but who still have children in the home)—the groups that middle-class, white churches have had the most success in attracting for many years. This is a pattern which is as old as suburbanization, and it continues today. The pattern may not be as strong as it was in the 1950s, but new housing is still a major factor in predicting church growth.

The independent effect of the percent of community residents who are black on church growth was very weak, while the independent effect of racial transition remained quite strong. This makes some sense. Percent of black residents is related both to the economic condition of the community and to the proportion of housing that is new. Racial transition, however, does not have much correlation with either two contextual variables. Many areas undergoing racial transition today are suburban, rather than inner city, and the economic status of black residents in a racially changing community typically is similar to that of the white residents whom they are replacing. For these reasons, the effect of racial transition is independent of other contextual variables; and because the typical white church does not adjust well to racial change, the negative effect on church membership can be substantial. When white Americans are able to accept African-Americans as neighbors or when churches become able to change along with their communities, the negative impact of racial transition on church growth within predominatly white denominations should disappear.

The economic status of the community also seems to have an independent effect on church growth, although it is not as strong as the impact of new housing or racial change. Southern Baptist congregations tend to be white and middle class. The same is true for most mainline denominations, other than the American Baptist Churches, which is a highly integrated denomination (its churches tend to be either predominantly black or predominantly white, however). For this reason, Southern Baptist churches tend to grow best in areas that are solidly middle class or even relatively affluent. Growth is much less likely in areas that are characterized by high rates of poverty and unemployment. Obviously this has nothing to do with the likelihood of "reaching the lost," but it has everything to do with growing a self-supporting institution. Still, it should be remembered that if conservative denominations follow the trend of the mainline churches and become steadily more affluent, they will find themselves competing for a dwindling resource. The growth of individual churches may be encouraged by affluent residents, but the growth of a denomination is encouraged by reaching the widest range of groups in the population, from poverty to affluence.

One aspect of the environment of a church which has nothing to do with the demographics of the area concerns a population of another sort—other churches of the same denomination. The proximity of such churches is related to growth, and the effect is negative. The closer the distance, the less likely a church is to see growth.

There are those who would argue that since churches have different purposes, and presumably reach different target audiences, that the presence of another church in close proximity should be irrelevant. This is not true in most cities and towns, however. It is typical for churches of the same denomination to be rather densely packed in older urban neighborhoods and in older suburban developments. At one time all of these congregations were doing well. New housing was being constructed at a rapid pace, neighborhoods were homogeneous and were well populated with many suburban churches. Nearly all grew, even when located within a mile of one another, and this encouraged the development of even more churches in these communities. When the population stopped growing, and when the neighborhoods became more heterogeneous, the churches found themselves competing for a dwindling resource—the traditional family with children in the home. Rather than survival of the fittest, in most cases all or nearly all of the churches in such areas plateaued or declined.

Finally, there is the issue of church age. Younger churches are more likely to grow than are older congregations. For younger churches this suggests that they should not congratulate themselves too much on their growth rates—because much of their growth results from what they *are*, rather than from what they are *doing*. These congregations should work to keep the social groups within their congregations open, so that as their church ages it will not suffer the typical fate of the middle-age church: a plateau in membership.

Older churches should not accept their age as something which precludes growth. Beyond fifty years or so, additional decades, or even centuries, do not matter. Older churches, whether fifty years of age or 250, tend to be closed fellowship composed of rigid social groups which do not readily accept new members. This pattern can be broken, however, and has been broken by churches which are approaching their 250th birthdays in New England.

Churches must understand their context, their competition, and their character. These factors are not irrelevant to church growth and must be considered in planning for change. They should not be viewed as deterministic, however. Unchangeable factors can be *exploited, overcome*, or *used* to shape the development of a more realistic identity. The church which does any of these three things, but especially the latter, will be stronger and more likely to succeed than the church which uses a tried and true formula for growth which supposedly is applicable to any church setting. This is unrealistic and ignorant from a planning perspective. A meaningful statement of purpose only can be developed with clear understanding of the present situation both inside and outside the walls of the church. And the development of a realistic new identity and the growth-producing goals which emerge from such an identity provide the only feasible way a nongrowing church will be able to transform itself into a growing congregation.